DRIFT

HAVANA

ADAM GOLDBERG
Editor in Chief

EDITORIAL   CREATIVE

ELYSSA GOLDBERG
Executive Editor

DANIELA VELASCO
Creative Director

BONJWING LEE
Copy Editor

JASON FITZ
Photographer

ALEXANDRA SVOKOS
Contributor

ANDREW COLE
Contributor

ANGELA ALMEIDA
Contributor

CLAIRE BOOBBYER
Contributor

CHRISTOPHER BAKER
Contributor

ELENA SHEPPARD
Contributor

JEVA LANGE
Contributor

JOHN SURICO
Contributor

KATE THORMAN
Contributor

KATHLYN CURTO
Contributor

RACHEL EVA LIM
Contributor

RICHARD FLEMING
Contributor

SARAH KOLLMORGEN
Contributor

WELCOME

I had always dreamed of visiting Havana. As an American, Cuba—the tropical island nation just 90 miles south of Florida—was mysterious. It's been off-limits to us for over 50 years, yet through the selectively porous walls of that economic embargo, I felt the lure of its seductive music and colorful, contemporary art.

I say selectively because that embargo made it virtually impossible to taste the country's dark, nutty, and chocolate-heavy coffee (or see the place). But now, with American-Cuban relations thawing, all of that is changing.

The story of Havana coffee over the last half-century has been one of perseverance: hacking together ingredients, equipment, and techniques to supplement a precipitous decrease in domestic production and screeching halt to foreign imports. Despite challenges in those decades, coffee brought citizens together, helping to assuage them in difficult times or reunite them in the best.

Make no mistake: Coffee culture in Havana is strong, and there are cafes, but there are no specialty coffee shops in Havana. Yet. Because a country of coffee lovers needs more than an affinity for the beverage to open small, independent businesses. It needs government backing and resources, a once-upon-a-time fantasy that may soon be a reality.

Volume 3 tells the story of what it's like to drink coffee in Havana—past and present, at home and in cafes, according to locals and *extranjeros*—in a city with a rapidly approaching, uncertain future on the edge of change.

We hope you'll pour yourself a cup and stay awhile.

ADAM GOLDBERG, *Editor in Chief*

TABLE OF CONTENTS

COCO TAXI

--

Writing by Elyssa Goldberg
Photo essay by Adam Goldberg

It looks more like a Disney World teacup on its side than it does transportation. But it's cheaper and more adorable than the glossy vintage Buicks without door handles (and quicker than a bicitaxi), so you'll take it anyway. Welcome to your Cocotaxi. Named for the half-coconut it resembles, the bright yellow-and-green automotive rickshaw scoots around town with tourists in tow. But it's in between stops, when drivers refuel *a lo Cubano*—stopping at the *ventanillas* scattered throughout the city and quickly downing *tazas de café*—that the whole operation slows down. Because even hustlers in Havana's dual economy need to refuel, and every driver has a favorite hangout.

ROLANDO GARCIA
September 13, 2015
Cafetería "Saint John's"

ALEXIS PAEZ
September 16, 2015
Cafetería Avenida Italia #513

IVAN MARTINEZ
September 16, 2015
Cafetería en la Feria de San José

GUILLERMO QUINTANA
September 17, 2015
Cafetería "El Cortez"

JOVANI MORA
September 16, 2015
Cafetería "Tu Parada"

FRANK VALDEZ
September 16, 2015
Cafetería "Mi Niña"

LEANDRO POSO
September 16, 2015
Cafetería "La Muralla"

THAEL FRANCO
September 13, 2015
Cafetería "La Familia"

"In the morning, all the taxi drivers line up here for coffee. We all know each other. We all work in this area and this is where we start our day."

"I like it *con leche*, with milk."

"It is a tradition. My mom roasts coffee and sells it to a cafetería. She roasts it with *chícharos* and adds sugar to change its color and make it shinier."

"I drink my coffee black, with no sugar so I can taste it."

"I drink it with my family every morning at breakfast, and also during the day when I smoke. I love the smell of it."

"I usually have coffee at home, but when I am working, My favorite is a *cortadito*"

"Cuban coffee is really good. Especially the one from *Oriente*."

"You know, when someone visits you at home the first thing you say is '*Vas a querer café?*'. It's a Cuban thing."

ORO NEGRO

--

Writing by Claire Boobbyer
Photography by Adam Goldberg

Greeting visitors at the no-frills cafe in the National Museum of Fine Arts in Havana is *La Cafedral*, a two meter-tall, tarnished silver cathedral fashioned from stacked Moka pots. The work of one of Cuba's most revered artists, Roberto Fabelo, it is an ode to the machine that brews coffee on the stove of every kitchen in Cuba, one that elevates the drink to a spiritual elixir.

And that's what coffee is in Cuba: the national drink; a conversation-starter; sweetener and succor for a storied Caribbean nation. Coffee, consumed morning through night in homes and on the street, fuels conversation where garrulous locals delight in out-talking each other and emphatically proving a point, where verbal dexterity in the *choteo*—the art of ribbing and an irreverent attitude—is a national skill indulged, practiced, and perfected by all Cubans.

If the modern-day visitor to Havana thinks that caffeinated Cuban linguistic marathons are a recent development, suggest the words of American explorer Alpheus Hyatt Verrill who penned a guidebook, the *Cuba of Today* in 1931, "The Cubans are great patronisers of the open-fronted cafes…talking and arguing as if they were responsible for the welfare of the world."

It wasn't always aromatic coffee, though, that perfumed each tropical dawn in this island nation. In early 18th-century Havana, chocolate was the breakfast beverage of choice. But the turmoil ravaging a neighboring island in the latter half of the 18th-century transformed the history, fortunes, and the drinking culture of Cuba.

When the French colonized the western part of the island of Hispaniola (now Haiti) in 1659, French planters cultivated coffee using West African slaves. But in the 1790s, thousands of slaves revolted, forcing French planters to flee to Cuba, many accompanied by their slaves.

In Santiago de Cuba and Guantánamo in Cuba's Oriente (the East)—the closest *terra firma* to western Hispaniola—officials granted thousands of settlers land concessions. It is thought that between 15,000 and 30,000 fled to Cuba. The planters farmed the land of the Oriente's Sierra Maestra mountains—in particular, establishing high altitude *cafetales*, or coffee plantations, of Arabica coffee.

Rewind a little further, and you'll see that the coffee bean's relationship with Cuba began earlier than the Hispaniola uprising, when a Don José Gelabert brought the bean to his estate in Wajay, outside Havana, in 1748. The idea of planting the bean spread and coffee was slowly scattered across the mountains of western and central Cuba, along with parts of the east. But it wasn't until the rapid proliferation of French plantations in El Oriente that coffee drinking began to filter through the salons of Tivolí, the French quarter of Spanish colonial Santiago de Cuba, and became embedded in the daily ritual in Cuba's second city.

It was fitting, then, that a Frenchman, Juan Bautista Tavern, founded the first coffee shop in Havana on the corner of Calles Mercaderes and Teniente Rey on Plaza Nueva (now elegant Plaza Vieja) in the early 1770s, according to Cuban journalist Rolando Aniceto. (Today, Tavern's coffeehouse is La Taberna, where expensive nightly live music shows entertain packs of tourists.)

At the time, Tavern sold young Cubans, curious for their first taste of the drink, 2.5 oz (71 g) of ground coffee diluted in a liter of boiling water—not too far off the modern day barista's ideal ratio of ground coffee to water, although far in excess of *un cafecito*, or Cuban-style espresso.

Home brewing appeared slow to catch on, for it wasn't until 1790, writes Ned Sublette in *Cuba and Its Music*, that Havana's first newspaper, *Papel Periódico de La Habana*, printed a recipe for brewing coffee in its first edition.

By the 1830s, Cuba's black gold output was at its peak. But the nascent coffee industry suffered a seismic shock as sugar, Cuba's white gold, was seen to be far more profitable than the aromatic bean. Across the island, *cafetales* were destroyed to make way for sugar plantations.

To note, coffee drinking—*con leche or solo*—by now, had become an indelible part of Cuban culture. In 1859, some 65 cafes served Havana including the Café de Copas, Café de los Franceses, La Dominicana, Marte y Belona, and Escauriza; by 1890, Havana boasted 156 coffee shops. Havana's golden age had come. Sugar was king and trading in white gold built up the magnificent and eclectic architectural landscape of the capital city.

As Havana grew fat and wealthy on sugar harvested by West African slaves, coffee culture downsized, with production ebbing and flowing through the first half of the 20th century.

Coffee production, nationalized after Fidel Castro's 1959 Cuban Revolution, has taken a hit in recent years. In the early 1990s, just before the Soviet Union's annual subsidies to Cuba ($3 billion annually) were amputated by the fall of communism in the USSR, Cuba produced almost 25 million kilograms of coffee, according to the International Coffee Organization. That number had sunk to just five and a half million kilos in 2009 to 2010 and has risen only slightly again over the last several years. This drastic plunge led the government to resort to unconventional measures.

The year 2011 became known as the *Año del café mezclado* as one joke went. A riff on the *Año 52 de La Revolución*, a date printed on all official material, 2011 marked the year the Cuban government resorted again to adding chickpeas into ground coffee (*café con chícharo*) to sell to Cubans in the bodegas, their neighborhood ration stores. Cubans buy 4 oz. of *café con chícharo* for 0.75CUP (US$0.03) via their monthly rations, or resort to the black market and pay 15 CUP (US$0.6) for the same packet. Determined coffee drinkers buy black market coffee beans that have been smuggled from the eastern provinces. Beans that survive the risky journey, having escaped the noses of policemen at roadside stops, must then be roasted and ground at home—pure dedication for pure *café*.

Yet Raúl Castro's late 2010 economic reforms, introduced to inject life into Cuba's moribund economy, have helped the Havana cafe scene flourish. Previously, with few exceptions, travelers had to rely on an espresso from state-run venues stripped of ambience and any semblance of service. But now, the busy streets are full of kiosks selling *buchitos* (*cafecitos*) to locals in pesos for 1 CUP, and privately owned (and stylish) coffee haunts for those with hard currency (CUCs) to spend. Café Mamainé, whose name embodies the spirit of one of Cuba's most famous personalities, is one of these new retreats. Every Cuban can sing the words of Eliseo Grenet's 1927 *Mama Inés* song, popularised by Cuban singing great Rita Montaner, with the catchy, immortal lines: *"Ay Mamá Inés, Ay Mamá Inés, todos los negros tomamos café."*

But it's probably *trova* singer Carlos Puebla, best known as the Singer of the Revolution, who synthesised best the meaning of a morning *demitasse* of coffee for *los Cubanos* in his song *Si No Fuera por Emiliana*. Paying homage to the sustenance of brewed Cuban coffee, its humble roots in the farmsteads of Cuba's *el campo*, or countryside, he sings of the necessity of having a *compañera* to offer you a *buchito* when the going gets tough.

Emiliana es una cubana que en el albergue es fundamental.	Emiliana is a Cuban who is fundamental to the home.
Emiliana es muy cumplidora, es halagadora, alegre y cordial.	Emiliana is very dutiful, is a flatterer, cheerful and friendly.
Emiliana no se demora y en la colada siempre es puntal	Emiliana does not delay, always filtering the coffee on time.
Si no fuera por Emiliana nos quedaríamos con las ganas,	If it were not for Emiliana, we would be without the desire,
de tomar café, de tomar café, de tomar café, de tomar café.	to drink coffee, to drink coffee, to drink coffee, to drink coffee.

■

CUBAN COFFEE: A PRIMER

--

Writing by Sarah Kollmorgen
Photography by Adam Goldberg and Daniela Velasco

Before the revolution, Cuba was a powerhouse in the global coffee community: Up until the mid-50s, the country was exporting up to 20,000 tons of premium coffee beans abroad and espresso machines brought over from Italy shaped creative Cuban variations on classic drinks like the espresso and cortado.

But the Cuban Revolution of 1959 and the years of economic stagnation that followed stunted coffee culture on the island. Exports of Cuban coffee beans plummeted, and the government curtailed local consumption by rationing coffee— two ounces per adult every two weeks. Yet the vibrant coffee culture that emerged pre-Cuban Revolution didn't die off completely in those hard times; instead, it percolated among Habaneros who stayed and traveled to the U.S. with those who left. To know and love Havana is to know its fundamental coffee drinks.

CAFÉ CUBANO

Also known as *cafecito* or a Cuban espresso, the sweet but strong *café Cubano* is the foundation for other iconic Cuban espresso drinks. Simply, a *Cubano* is a shot of espresso infused with sugar—that is, the sugar is added and brewed into the coffee. This process makes the drink not only sweet, but viscous. Due to its potency, *Cubanos* are often served alongside a small cup of water.

The *Cubano* made its debut shortly after Italian espresso machines arrived in Cuba. *Cubanos* can also be made at home using a Moka pot. Once a little bit of coffee begins to percolate in the Moka pot, just a few drops are poured over a layer of sugar in the bottom of a small coffee cup. This sugar-coffee concoction, the *espumita*, is stirred like crazy until a light brown paste forms. The remaining coffee is then poured over this paste. Done correctly, the *espumita*, now a thin, caramel-colored layer will sit atop the *Cubano*.

Despite their strength, these little cups are best enjoyed in the afternoon, rather than in the morning. Served in small cups, *Cubanos* are consumed everywhere and by everyone—by passersby at a neighbor's *ventanilla* and by tourists at local coffee shops around town.

COLADA

The *colada* would be the social butterfly of the Cuban espresso family. While a *Cubano* is a single shot of espresso, a *colada* contains anywhere from three to six shots, and is expected to be shared. A *colada* is usually served in a larger Styrofoam cup and doled out into little plastic cups. Individual portions are taken on-the-go. *Coladas* have become a staple of Cuban communities abroad, particularly in Miami, Florida.

CARAJILLO

A *carajillo* is a *café Cubano* with an added kick. Traditionally a Spanish drink, the *carajillo* combines coffee with rum, brandy, or whiskey. In Cuba, rum is the liquor of choice. Ask Habaneros whether they restrict carajillo consumption to the afternoon, and they'll scoff: It may be boozy, but a *carajillo* should be enjoyed anytime morning, noon, or night.

CAFÉ CRIOLLO

Café criollo refers to a method guajiros, or those who live in Cuba's vast countryside, developed to brew coffee using a *manga*. A *manga* is a thick cloth, a sock-like filter that allows for a pour-over extraction method, rather than brewing with a Moka pot or espresso machine the way most city-dwellers do. Some Habaneros swear that guajiros won't even touch coffee without first dripping it through la *manga*.

CAFÉ CON LECHE

The *café con leche* is the black sheep of the family, as it's made without a sweetened espresso shot. It's also a D.I.Y. drink: A shot of espresso is served alongside a cup of hot or steamed milk, and coffee-drinkers add as much espresso and sugar to the milk as they deem fit. This creates a rich, creamy, and thick drink, often had at breakfast with a side of *tostadas*, or Cuban toast.

CAFÉ BOMBÓN

Originally from Spain, the *bombón* is a showy drink. Sweetened condensed milk is carefully poured into a shot of espresso, in equal parts, until the milk sinks to the bottom of the glass to create a chic, thick, and extra-sweet drink. In Havana, a *bombón* may be served in a Champagne flute for ultimate visual effect, because when the coffee separates from the condensed milk, it appears as distinct black and white layers.

CORTADITO

The *cortadito* is the *Cubano*'s less intense younger brother: It's a *Cubano* topped off with steamed milk. Like the Italian cortado, milk is added to create a smoother—but still strong—drink. The amount of milk added to a *cortadito* varies recipe to recipe, but it's generally a ratio of one-to-one or three-to-one milk to espresso. Unlike a cortado, a *cortadito* is pre-sweetened.

WALKING TO GUANTANAMO

--

Writing by Richard Fleming
Photography by Adam Goldberg

It was on my very first afternoon in Havana that I began to understand that, in Cuba, coffee is the currency of hospitality. After a steamy flight in a vintage Soviet-made jet and a harrowing experience passing through customs, I finally arrived at a grand Victorian mansion in the Vedado district, where I was met by a kindly grandmother renting her home out as a *casa particular*. "Would you like coffee?" were the first friendly words spoken to me in the country.

I had arrived with the half-baked, and, in retrospect, almost demented idea that I would walk from one end of the island to the other, experiencing the everyday life of Cubans. It was the very end of the Special Period, a long era of necessity and adjustment to the realities of the post-Soviet order; more than ten years earlier, the USSR had simply ceased to exist, leaving basic necessities like soap and matches essentially unobtainable. Yet the natural hospitality of Cubans was in constant tension with this profound scarcity; everywhere I went, the people I met were quick with a "*Quieres tomar café?*"

The offer of a coffee in Cuba is a gesture of friendship. It's a way of saying to visitors "we want, literally, to share our culture with you." It is served short, black, and sweet, and I drank many as I trudged across the country. During that four-month journey, Havana was my port in the storm, a place I circled back to whenever the solitude of walking alone through the countryside overwhelmed me (or when I needed to renew my visa). But it wasn't until my journey was almost complete that I stumbled across a strange family group of musicians performing at the Festival del Caribe in Santiago de Cuba, that I saw just how close to the center of Cuban life the reverent preparation of coffee could be.

I came upon the band one evening onstage in a city park, playing slow, deliberate, antique music, something like a twisted, percussive, Napoleonic square dance. The instruments included an accordion, a single-string jug band bass, and the rattling jawbone of a donkey for percussion. Onstage, one woman danced as if alone in her kitchen, without any self-consciousness whatsoever. It was a tableau worthy of David Lynch: the music melancholy and dirgelike, the dancer lost in her own world, almost ecstatic and transported by the mild rhythms. It was like nothing I had ever heard before, and I was captivated.

As soon as their set was over, I hurried around the park and made my way behind the stage. "I love your music," I gushed to the first band member I came across.

"We are very unhappy with the performance," he said. "What you saw is not the whole spectacle. We didn't have the coffee, and a *moledor*."

"Coffee? You mean to drink?" *Moledor* was a word I didn't know.

He mimed the beating of coffee beans in a mortar. "Usually, while we play, the women make coffee. First, they grind the beans, then they carefully mix in the *guarapo* before they cook the coffee." *Guarapo*, I knew, was sugarcane juice. "Then they serve it to the audience while we are playing. We play so that the women will be happy while they work. Without them making it for us, we are uninspired. The music is not the same." This description sounded even more surreal and wonderful than the spectacle I had just witnessed.

"We have all been depressed by this since we arrived." he said. His name was Francisco Escalona, and he told me that the band was called Guasimal. "We talked to the festival organizers several times to explain the situation but they still haven't been able to get the coffee we need."

I scribbled down their festival schedule and promised to go and see them at their next gig. "I hope you get the coffee," I said.

The next day at the Union of Artists and Writers, the band took the stage in front of an intimate crowd of fifteen, afternoon beer-drinking intellectuals. I sat at a table on the little patio and waved hello to Francisco. The presenter explained that the band existed only as part of the Escalona-Rodriguez family ritual of making coffee, but that, unfortunately, there was no coffee to be had because of Cuba's difficult situation. "Normally," he said, "the coffee would be ground in time to the music, with rhythmic strokes, and sweetened with *guarapo*."

During the show, the dazzling yet unknowable pregnant woman with the enigmatic smile again danced with herself, performing for the handful of people on the patio with just as much spirit and enthusiasm as she had for the much larger crowd in the plaza. Solely by virtue of having come see them perform again, we were now friends. During the set, the presenter came and joined me.

"Incredible stuff, isn't it?" he asked. He was a man about town, wiry and savvy with greasy salt-and-pepper hair. "It's music that hasn't changed in a hundred years."

"There's something strange and wonderful about them," I said.

"There are thousands of questions about this band to which I don't have the answer. Have you seen them do their thing with the coffee?"

"Unfortunately not."

"You must see that to get the whole experience. Apparently, there was some screwup. The festival was going to provide the coffee but now they say the band should have brought their own." ▶ ▶ ▶

"How much does coffee cost, anyway?" I asked, looking up at the stage. "I love how she dances."

"You're in for a disappointment, then: they're only dancing because there's no coffee. Normally, the women would be working the whole time to prepare it."

After another sublime set, Francisco and Angel Escalona came down from the stage and joined us. "You were great again," I said.

"Well, thanks," said Francisco, "but I didn't think so. We're a little tense because of the problems with the coffee. We're leaving in three days and still haven't done our complete spectacle."

"Why don't you look for someone *with possibilities* to help you get some?" asked the presenter, all but jerking his thumb in my direction.

This went right past Angel and Francisco. They were far too country to pick up this unsubtle hint. The presenter raised his eyebrows meaningfully a couple of times while I envisioned the damage a twenty-kilo burlap sack of premium Sierra Madre coffee beans would do to my backpacker budget. I squirmed uncomfortably, but Francisco shrugged his shoulders. He knew nobody with possibilities.

"Maybe tomorrow they'll have some for us," he said.

"I wouldn't count on it," said the presenter. He opened his eyes wide and stared straight at me. "*Mira*, think carefully. I really think you could find someone. Maybe a foreigner. *With possibilities*." We both laughed a bit nervously. To my amazement, Angel and Francisco still had no idea what the presenter was suggesting.

"I might be able to help," I said at last. "How much coffee would you need?"

"Let me ask." Francisco called over the divine dancer.

"How much coffee is required?" I asked her. By then I had warmed up to the idea.

"Just a little bit, a handful. Just so we have some to demonstrate. One packet of ground coffee would be fine. We can put it in the mortar and pretend to grind it up." Even after almost four months in Cuba, I was staggered that all this stress and anxiety might have been relieved with a small bag of coffee.

I announced that I'd be honored to purchase a two hundred-gram packet of ground coffee for the band to use during its last performances. We agreed to meet the next afternoon at a small park at the uphill end of the

old city. When I arrived, the group was waiting for me; nearby was a place where coffee might be available for purchase. It was something like a cafe. We waited outside on the sidewalk while Francisco went in and began an interminable negotiation. I knew he was explaining the band's predicament in excruciating detail. At last, he emerged. "It's quite irregular, the guy says," he said. "They really just serve cups of coffee here. Brewed. But he's going to help us out."

I cut to the bottom line: "How much?"

"*Pues*, one dollar will get us what we need." I handed him a dollar. The rest of the Escalonas and Rodriguezes and I waited while Francisco went back in and completed the under-the-counter transaction.

That night, at the legendary *Casa de la Trova*, I was treated like a VIP. When the band arrived, I was standing in the back, watching one of a string of amazing bands. Angel Escalona escorted me to the front row, to a seat they had reserved. The radiant, dancing woman waved to me. She was fussing with a small portable stove, and as the band played, she put an enormous aluminum mug of water on to boil. The women pretended to grind the already ground coffee, pounding it in the *moledor*, a wooden mortar and pestle almost waist-high. They pulled down on the arm of the *guarapo* squeezer, tugging at a long lever that crushed a rod of fresh sugar cane until the sweet, beige juice dribbled down through a dugout slot carved into a chunk of tree. The audience, seated in rows at the rather staid Casa de la Trova, had no idea what to think. They were rapt.

Just as the water was coming to a boil the women stirred in the cane juice and then steeped the coffee with a long, brown-stained coffee sock. The music accompanying this extended ritual was bouncy and up-tempo. The tunes were the same ones I had already heard at the other gigs. But surfing along on the magnificent coffee aroma and waves of mutual love and support that were emanating from both sides of the stage, the music lost its melancholy, Lynchian quality of antique darkness. The presence of the coffee made the men happy, and they played with more energy, as if they had already drunk it.

As the audience applauded, the dancer brought me the very first serving. It would be wrong not to write that it was the best cup of coffee I've ever had. ∎

©Richard Fleming 2008/2015
Derived from Chapter 23 of Walking to Guantánamo,
prepared for Drift Magazine, 8/30/15

A KIWI IN CUBA:
Q&A WITH GEOFF MARSLAND

--

Writing by Rachel Eva Lim
Photography by Daniela Velasco

Coffee has been an essential part of New Zealander Geoff Marsland's life for the past two decades. His Wellington-based roasting company, Havana Coffee Works, has been importing green coffee from Cuba since 1997 and remains the only Kiwi organization to do so. After a fateful visit to a cafe in Vancouver, Canada, nearly three decades ago, Marsland was inspired to create a coffee-centric community hub back home. Together with his business partner, Tim Rose, Marsland founded Havana Midnight Espresso—cheekily named for its Cuba Street location—in Wellington in 1988, and followed it with another cafe, Havana Deluxe, three months later. To keep up with the coffee demand of their two businesses, ensure the quality of their beans, and live up to their establishments' names, Marsland and Rose decided to enter the roasting market by opening Havana Coffee Works and sourcing a significant amount of their beans from Cuba.

Though Marsland and Rose's first trip to Havana coincided with a grim recession triggered by Russia's economic withdrawal from the country, the pair was able to forge a lasting relationship with the Cuban government. Today, they import around six shipping containers full of green coffee each year. The beans, transported to New Zealand on a three month journey via the Panama Canal, are then roasted locally using a modified electric Petroncini hot air coffee roaster. Here, Marsland talks about why Cuban coffee is worth the trouble, how selling tie-dye on tour with the Grateful Dead helped shape his coffee future, and what it's like to share a cup of joe with Cuban officials.

What were your experiences with coffee like before you started Havana Coffee Works?
It all began when I spent a season selling tie-dye on tour with the Grateful Dead in 1987. I used to sell my tie-dye in London and people on the street would tell me that the Grateful Dead would love my stuff—so I took my big bag of tie-dye to Los Angeles, bought a huge yank tank [slang for a 1950s or 1960s American car], found out where the Grateful Dead were and ended up traveling along the West Coast with them. They were playing with people like Jimmy Cliff, Robert Cray, and Bob Dylan, and there were about 25 tie-dye stores that traveled with them. I used to call myself Nuclear Free Clothing and my tie-dye was totally unique; people really loved it, so it ended up being a really successful trip.

After the tour ended I went to Vancouver where I visited a little coffee shop called Joe's Café on Commercial Drive. I hung out there, just drinking coffee and eating doughnuts with all sorts of different people. I absolutely loved it, and I thought, "I'm going to go back and do this in New Zealand!" I bought a coffee machine right there and then, shipped it home with my mate, and told all my friends I was going to open a coffee shop. So, in 1988, Tim and I opened Havana Midnight Espresso in the middle of Cuba Street, which I later found out was named after a ship called Cuba that used to transport coffee to New Zealand in the 1840s.

Why did you start importing Cuban coffee beans into New Zealand?
Now that we had our own coffee roaster I thought, "Shit, I'm gonna go and find the best coffee in the world." So, in 1991, I jumped on a plane and went to Jamaica. The coffee was so expensive. Then I realized Cuba was right next door. I wrote to the Cubans, and Tim and I flew to Havana in 1997, which was when we imported our first container of Cuban coffee. We were young, only in our twenties, when we first visited Havana, and it was such an amazing place where it's so easy to just get caught up in the romance of the city itself. It felt like going to the moon.

What do you love about Cuban coffee?
I've been working in coffee for 26 years and I think that, to put it in simple terms, coffee is like the place it comes from. Indonesian coffee is very gnarly and Cuban coffee is like the music, rum, and cigars. It's, ooh la la!—absolutely delicious.

There are roughly three different growing areas and about four or five grades of Cuban coffee. The highest one is called Crystal Mountain, which is just a step below Jamaican Blue Mountain. The Japanese buy almost all the Crystal Mountain, but I manage to snag a little bit of it. Then there's Extra Turquino Lavado, Lavado, and Super Serrano, which are all from different regions. I've been able to taste each of them, and they're all just beautiful.

Can you talk a little about the logistics of importing coffee from Cuba to New Zealand?
In New Zealand, we've never had any trade restrictions with Cuba, but the Americans have given us lots of problems. They've said that we're trading with the enemy or that we're terrorists, and our money's gone missing multiple times. So, it's been a real problem getting our payments through to the Cubans because the Americans would freeze our cash transfers,

which meant that our shipments would miss the boat to New Zealand. The Cubans themselves have been amazing to deal with, but the Americans have made it very difficult.

How have your interactions been like with the Cuban government?
The Cuban government has been absolutely wonderful. When we first went to Havana we brought along suitcases full of foreign coffee to show them in order to prove that we were legit. But we initially had it all confiscated at the airport and had to explain who we were, where New Zealand was, and what we were doing. Once the government officials found out what we had, they rushed over to meet us at the airport, because they'd never experienced high quality coffee from places other than Cuba before. We took our coffee to their government department in Havana; it has these massive marble floors, big boardroom tables, and huge photos of Che Guevara everywhere. They have a room where they work with their exporters. We went inside, sat at a cupping table with them, and watched them sample the Columbian, Kenyan, and Ethiopian coffees we brought. Gathering like that with these government guys in their sixties who've lived in Cuba and worked in coffee their entire lives was just a magical experience. And when Tim and I finally got to taste the Cuban coffee they had, we thought, "Oh, we've won the lottery!"

What have you learned about the industry over the years?
The coffee growing industry in Cuba is pretty closed. It isn't somewhere like Colombia where you can come as a tourist and just visit the plantations and stuff. In Cuba, it's not like that. They don't let you go into the processing plants. They're lovely people and everything, but it's still a pretty closed economy and their system is very old-school.

What's your relationship like with the farmers, then?
The best part of all this has just been the really human experience of interacting with them, especially back in the early days. When we started importing coffee in the 1990s there were very few visitors going to coffee plantations around the world and interacting with the coffee growers. Now every man and his dog goes to visit the origins and buys a suitcase of coffee—that's how you get to call yourself a coffee importer—but back then it was really rare for a coffee farmer to meet the end user. It was a wonderful experience for us to go to Cuba, to be able to talk to these people about New Zealand, to bring toys for their kids and to have the opportunity to sit around with people from different cultures and generations, playing music and eating together after a long day of harvesting coffee. It was just such a pinch-yourself experience.

Knowing what you know about Cuba, what do you see for the future?
There's already a coffee shortage in Cuba. Plus, there's a lack of money and a bad economy that's compounded by the fact that everything is run through the government departments. The Cubans haven't had enough money to put any nutrients back into the soil or to keep investing in the plantations. It's definitely a worry for me. I've already had other people in America contacting me, trying to bypass the trade restrictions by buying Cuban coffee from me. I'm worried that the Americans are gonna be trying to get all our coffee! But I'm also hoping that the Cubans remember the people, like us, who've been with them since the early days. ∎

IRRATIONAL

--

Writing by Angela Almeida and John Surico
Photography by Adam Goldberg and Daniela Velasco

"Che Guevara had a dream of a free Cuba," Rigoberto says, shaking the flimsy railing flanking the staircase of an apartment building along Calle Muralla. "This is not the dream he had."

We met Rigoberto earlier that day in Plaza Vieja, en route to Café El Escorial. He stopped us outside, before we could enter into what many locals told us was a tourist-only destination, a European-style cafe that sells specialty coffee at prices out of reach to the average Cuban. Rigoberto promised to show us the "real Cuba."

That's how, a few blocks later, we found ourselves at the rations *bodega*.

A large blackboard that reads "*Pizarra De Distribución*" hangs in the background of the small, dimly lit food store. It lists what is available for October, with items like rice, milk, salt, beans, and olive oil on this month's menu. Nearby, a sparsely stocked shelf is lined with individual water bottles, repurposed as containers for the menu items. Each is labeled with the corresponding price per weight. When we arrive, a kilo of coffee fills one water bottle and will cost Habaneros four national pesos.

Meanwhile, Cubans at the counter carry their rations book—known as a *libreta*—in hand, waiting to find out what's left.

Open seven days a week, a rations *bodega* can be found on nearly every block in Cuba's capital. It is one of the most visible vestiges of the revolution—a symbol of the egalitarian society that Fidel Castro strove to create, one that ensures all citizens, both rich and poor, have enough to eat for that month. At least in theory.

Since its inception in 1962, the ration system has been a street-level indicator of the larger Cuban economy. What is sold inside of the *bodegas* reflects what Cuba can import, or what the country already has on hand. So, when Cuba lost its most integral international supplier relationship with the fall of the Soviet Union in 1991, the rations lessened, as the country entered a deep recession.

Since then, the ongoing trade embargo with the United States, coupled with a lack of domestic agricultural production, has forced the Cuban government to look elsewhere for food—like the faraway land of Vietnam, where most Cuban rice now comes from, a costly alternative for a country where the staple dish is *arroz y frijoles*. So, as the price of food products continues to increase, the country has had to grapple with less.

That reality is felt in the rations.

"If you look inside the fish shops, all you'll see are stacks of eggs," Rigoberto remarks, noting how little fish there is to sell. "And if you look in the markets, all you'll find is pork."

For the 11 million Cubans who depend on the state-subsidized rations, it's a numbers game, one that is visibly stacked against them. The average state wage is still less than $20 a month, with 80 percent of it reportedly spent on food. But the system is weakening, as the rations themselves grow scarce. Each passing year, the rations *bodega* more fully represents something else: what is barely available to Cubans, and what is readily consumed by tourists.

"When I took a group of Americans on a tour three months ago, they brought me out to dinner, and I had steak," Reinaldo, a cab driver, says, with longing. We asked him when he had last tasted beef. "I can't even remember."

You'll never find beef in a butcher shop here. All cows are said to be state property, including those held on private ranches. Reinaldo said his father, who owns dairy cows, must burn them if they die rather than eat them. If caught illegally cooking beef, Cubans face up to 18 years in prison—more time in jail than a murder conviction.

Then, there's lobster. Manuel, a university student, jokes that langosta is "the cousin of shrimp I can't have." Police often patrol the coastlines, checking fishermen's cars for the prized possession, since lobsters are strictly reserved for tourists and exports. The fine for being caught is 2,000 CUC ($2,000), an amount unthinkable to most Cubans.

Yet the menus at tourist-friendly restaurants are littered with images of the buttered crustacean. At the Havana airport later in the week, before our flight home, one American visitor gleefully remarked, "I can't believe how cheap they are here!"

Milk is also notably scant, and, if available, expensive. One visitor from Barbados, Roland, said that when he recently visited Havana for business, he was never approached for money. Instead, after one Cuban woman helped him with directions, she asked Roland to pay her back with something else. "All she wanted was a gallon of milk," he said. ▶▶▶

Other items are vanishing off the shelves of rations *bodegas*, too. Potatoes and peas were discontinued in 2009. Soap, detergent, and cigarettes are long gone. When we visited the *bodegas*, the slots beside cigars, matches, and chickpeas were left blank.

But these gradual reductions are, by no means, unintentional—instead, they're indicative of a change in power. Since assuming Fidel's leadership role in 2008, Raúl Castro, his little brother, has grown harshly critical of rations, citing them as "an unbearable burden for the economy and a disincentive to work."

And, at least on the cost of it all, perhaps he has a point. Just to keep up with domestic demand, the Cuban government must import nearly 80 percent of its food, costing the state $2 billion a year. Not to mention that the Cuban government spends upwards of $1 billion in subsidies to make the rations affordable to its citizens.

Even while some supporters argue that rationing provides a vital safety net for the poorest Cubans, the younger Castro has essentially argued that, rather than rely on rations, the Cubans who can shop elsewhere for their food should, leaving the welfare program to better assist poorer Cubans who really need it. As a result, Castro has begun dismantling the age-old institution. The disappearing inventory in the *bodegas*, therefore, is a deliberate attempt to wean the citizenry off what Raul sees as a burden.

And coffee could be next on his chopping block.

The Cuban government is rumored to be considering cutting off the caffeine-packed lifeline of its people. While the country was harvesting 60,000 tons of coffee 50 years ago, production has drastically dropped to less than 6,000 tons in recent years. To meet demands, the Cuban government has had to spend upwards of $40 million to import coffee beans from other countries.

To think: Cuba, a country once renowned for its coffee, now needs to import it.

It is a pattern that has become all too familiar to locals. Even though coffee still remains a fixture in Cuban households, the news of the possible cut evokes shrugs, not rage. "If that happens, there won't be protests," Victor, a waiter, explains. "We don't scream here."

Like most other products from the *bodegas*, a kilo of coffee is meant for the month, but is actually only good for about ten days. This is also why government-regulated coffee is cut with what is known as chícharo, a roasted chickpea mixture, to create a blend with one purpose: to last.

The idea of eventually getting rid of rations would be to force Cubans to seek alternatives. But, in the case of coffee, that means Cubans can either sip it in cafes, or buy bags at the *mercados*, which are priced at nearly $7, a roughly 240 percent markup from rationed coffee. The unfortunate reality is that both are luxuries that the average Cuban cannot afford.

So many are readjusting.

Some, like Reinaldo, prefer driving Western tour groups around the city, hoping for a tip that could last them days. Others, like Manuel, have taken to Airbnb, an online service through which visitors can book lodging, including for *casas particulares* and short-term rental apartments. And if you ask any tourist walking the streets of Havana recently, they'll likely tell you about a self-proclaimed 'personal' tour guide who promised cigars straight from the factory and the best *comida cubana* along the Malecón. All he or she asked for was 10 CUC or so.

For Rigoberto, his career as a construction worker wasn't enough to pay the bills. To make extra money, he became a tattoo artist; the tourists he services pay him in CUC, the currency predominantly established for tourists that outweighs the Cuban peso (CUP) 25 to one. Most consumer goods on the market are priced in CUC now—not the national currency—further cementing the growing divide.

Ultimately, these workarounds are a product of a country that's developing faster than its means of living, a country where the hustle has replaced the revolutionary rallying cry *Hasta La Victoria Siempre—Until Victory, Always*—as the prevailing spirit of the people. But what citizens are buying is not necessarily the promise of a new Cuba, just the hope that they'll be able to survive here. ∎

*The last names of subjects were omitted to protect their identities.

RECLAIMED: Q&A WITH DAMIAN AQUILES

--

Interview and photography by
Adam Goldberg and Daniela Velasco

Handcut metal men march single-file across a wall. They're made from salvaged car parts and machinery scraps, whatever materials Damian Aquiles could get his hands on. When visual artist Damian Aquiles isn't traveling the world or mingling with the biggest names in the art and fashion worlds, he's in his studio in Havana, creating. Here, Aquiles shares what it's like to be an artist representing Havana on the international stage and how, with a bottomless *cafetera* at his side, he fuels his work.

Tell us a bit about yourself.
I am from Jaruco, a place about 50 minutes away from Havana. I studied graphic design and then painting. I've been painting for a long time. I took classes since I was a kid and have been diving into it ever since. Then something changed; I just used what I learned from design and began to use it in my pieces. I love graphic design, but when you do it, you are constrained to whatever your customer wants. By comparison, as a painter and sculptor I get to do whatever I want to do, and customers either value and love it or not. Either way, I get to do my own thing.

How did you first get into art?
For as long as I can remember, I've always wanted to be a painter. When I was 17, I decided I was going to be one for sure. Of course I didn't really know what that meant or where I wanted to get to. Because it's one thing to want to be a painter, it's another one to become one, and then another thing entirely to succeed at being one. From wanting to paint to selling paintings, there is a long, long way to go.

How would you characterize your art?
I use materials that have already been used, materials that have had another life, materials that I've found. I don't call it recycling; I call it working with the memory of the material. It can be wood, textile, cans, you name it—but I usually use metals, items that were created for a different initial use. I recontextualize them before incorporating them into my art. If there is a stain, or if it used to be a paint tin and has a dripping stain, I try to use it as part of my piece rather than try to remove it.

What role do those salvaged materials play in your work?
Cubans try to retain their things or properties. For instance, if someone has an old sofa, and they can restore it, they'll restore it instead of throwing it out. In other countries, if something gets old, they throw it out and get a new one. In Cuba, you try to keep your items functioning for as long as possible.

How does that mindset factor into your art, if at all?
I don't try to make my pieces Cuban. I mean, I am Cuban, but I try to make it international. I don't want it to only be Cuban. For instance, if I'm in Mexico or Spain or Brazil—wherever—and I find cans or materials that are interesting, I'll work with those instead.

What's the art community like in Havana?
During the revolution, there was a cultural movement that built schools for music, dance, liberal arts, theater, and other artistic endeavors. That provided some sort of background. If you build and teach art, dance, and theater to everyone, 40 years later you'll have an army of artists, dancers, and the like. The revolution dedicated a lot of time and effort into teaching sports, and culture.

Is there a large international market for Cuban art?
Especially in the United States there is a huge appetite for Cuban art. In fact, important collectors that have been purchasing art from places like China and Africa are now gearing their interest towards Cuban art instead. ▶▶▶

Are most of your buyers Cuban or foreign?

I get customers from all over. Mostly Americans, British, Spaniards, Mexicans, and some French. I've been getting considerably more interest from Americans lately too.

One thing you couldn't work without.

I can't start without coffee. I wake up, and I have coffee. It is the tool that gets me going. Coffee is like the first step. The caffeine wakes me up, of course. My employees always ask in the morning, "Have you had your coffee yet? Are you fully awake?" When I don't drink coffee, I just don't feel the same. I even bring the coffee I drink here with me when I travel. Of course, I always try whatever coffee is offered in the city I am visiting, but I always like to bring mine [Café Serrano] with me.

Do you drink coffee while you're working on your pieces then?

Yes, I drink it when I wake up and I drink it throughout the day. It's a ritual: I drink coffee if someone comes over; when I take breaks with my employees; and to stay up when I need to work until late.

In the United States and elsewhere, coffee shops can be places to meet other artists and hang out. People sometimes treat them as offices too. Does that happen in Havana?

In Cuba, there is no such thing yet. Artists work in their studios or their houses. Hopefully, we'll get some nice coffee shops and that will start to appear over here soon. What we do now is invite people over to our houses for coffee instead. For instance, you come over, we talk, we drink coffee, you see my art, and so on. We just don't have coffee shop culture like that here yet.

Do you think coffee shop culture like that will ever have a place in Havana?

Yes, I think the city is almost ready for it. There are many people I know that have been thinking about opening coffee shops. I think it's just a matter of time. A friend of mine opened a place, not really a coffee shop, but a place you can go to order coffee; he serves coffee and tacos, among other things. I think that in three or four years, cafe culture like that is going to be a thing. People are already bouncing those ideas around.

Where do Cubans most often drink coffee?

You go to any Cuban's house and they'll offer you coffee. No matter how bad it is, or whether they give you the one mixed with peas, they will always offer coffee. Sometimes the mix with chickpeas can even be quite good, eh?

How do you prepare your coffee at home?

I like espresso, around two or three ounces. We use a *cafetera*, the metal mini coffee maker—you know, that Italian contraption you see everywhere here.

Where do you look for inspiration?

I don't think it is about inspiration anymore; this is my job. It is about loving an idea and pushing through. I wake up and need to work on a piece of art either with or without inspiration. I need to organize myself, create a schedule, and get to work. There are days when you feel more productive and you get more done, and days when you are less productive, so it takes you longer to finish. For instance, now, we are running around because we have a deadline for this coming week and we have to leave time for fixing errors, mounting the works, and seeing what could be improved. All of that has to happen before showing anything to the clients. Coffee helps with that. ■

THROUGH THE VENTANILLA

--

Writing by Elyssa Goldberg
Photography by Adam Goldberg and Daniela Velasco

The sun rises. Balcony doors crack open as laundry sways to the first sounds of roosters crowing, vintage cars sputtering, and reggaeton-playing boomboxes powering up. After just a few hours of sleep, Havana comes alive. And everyone needs their *café*.

Habaneros who don't get their fix at home grab cups on the go but not in the traditional sense. There are no to-go cups of coffee in Cuba—branded, packaged, or otherwise. These commuters take their morning coffee at *ventanillas*, windows of residential homes that open to sell coffee. Rigged with wobbly planks of wood for makeshift countertops and handwritten cardboard signs that read "*CAFÉ*" to lure passersby, these coffee shops are temporary. In New York, they'd be called pop-ups. But in Cuba, *ventanillas*—usually open from 6 am to 5 pm daily—are just another way to make a living.

"They say we're socialist, that everyone is equal," a friend, Yolanda Hernández Álvarez, shares. "But that's not true. There are differences." Specific needs of millions of Cubans can't possibly all be met by the state. For example, the soap offered at Álvarez's local, state-run distribution center dries out her skin, so she gets her soap from the market across the street instead. Then there are financial differences: Some Habaneros pick up side jobs driving bicitaxis or manning *ventanillas*. Others receive money transfers from family members abroad.

At the corner of Villegas and Lamparilla in Habana Vieja, José Bosqué and his wife serve coffee through the wrought iron gates of their ground floor flat for one *moneda nacional* a cup. They opened their *ventanilla* a month ago to make extra money. Though they needed a food vendor license to sell the *café mezclado* they brew in a *cafetera*, Bosqué's wife says it's worth it: "It's an investment." They'll start by serving coffee, but that license and the growing customer base it will build, sets them up to sell bread and other products down the line. Coffee was just the most economical way to start.

A bicitaxi driver lingering outside of a *ventanilla* at Aguacate and Obrapia swears that the particular home-brew at 270 Aguacate is the city's best. Or, at least, it's good enough that he drives by three, four, even five times a day to down a *demitasse*. While some *ventanillas* pour coffee from a large thermos into Dixie cups, this one trusts its customers with tiny and colorful ceramic mugs—no small feat, considering the owner says she sells close to 250 cups of coffee each day.

"Very sweet and very delicious," is how that bicitaxi driver describes the cup. And that's not surprising, considering *ventanilla* owners mix sugar into the coffee, which is almost always *café con chícharo*, before it's served.

A man drinking his morning cup elsewhere in Vieja notes that you can always add more sugar, if you want. But he likes the way Cafeteria la Estrella, a *ventanilla* with a jazzy name (and his favorite), at Aguacate and Muralla, serves its coffee: not too bitter, not too sweet. "I come to this one because it's better than the others," he says, ribbing on other *ventanilla* coffee as "water with the essence of *café*."

Another woman doling out coffee at her *ventanilla* at Sol and Villegas knows what she's doing. She mixes the sugar into the coffee in advance and tries to edge ahead of her competitors by offering Coffee Mate. She has regulars who come every morning, and she knows them all by name. When asked about her peak hours, she shrugs, "Most people here consume coffee all day long." ∎

*The last names of subjects were omitted to protect their identities.

CAFETERIA

Milanesa

CAFE	$1.00
REFRESCO GASEADO	2.00
REFRESCO	1.00
PAN c TORTILLA	5.00
PAN " PERRO	$7.00

EXTRACURRICULAR

--

Writing by Kathryn Curto
Photography by Adam Goldberg and Daniela Velasco

On most American college campuses, walking two or three blocks in any direction from the quad will land you on the doorstep of a coffee shop. But at the University of Havana and Instituto Superior de Artes (ISA), coffee's importance in student life has little to do with campus at all. While students find strong *cafés Cubanos* at artists' studios, conference rooms, and professors' offices, for university students studying in Havana, coffee is a reminder of home.

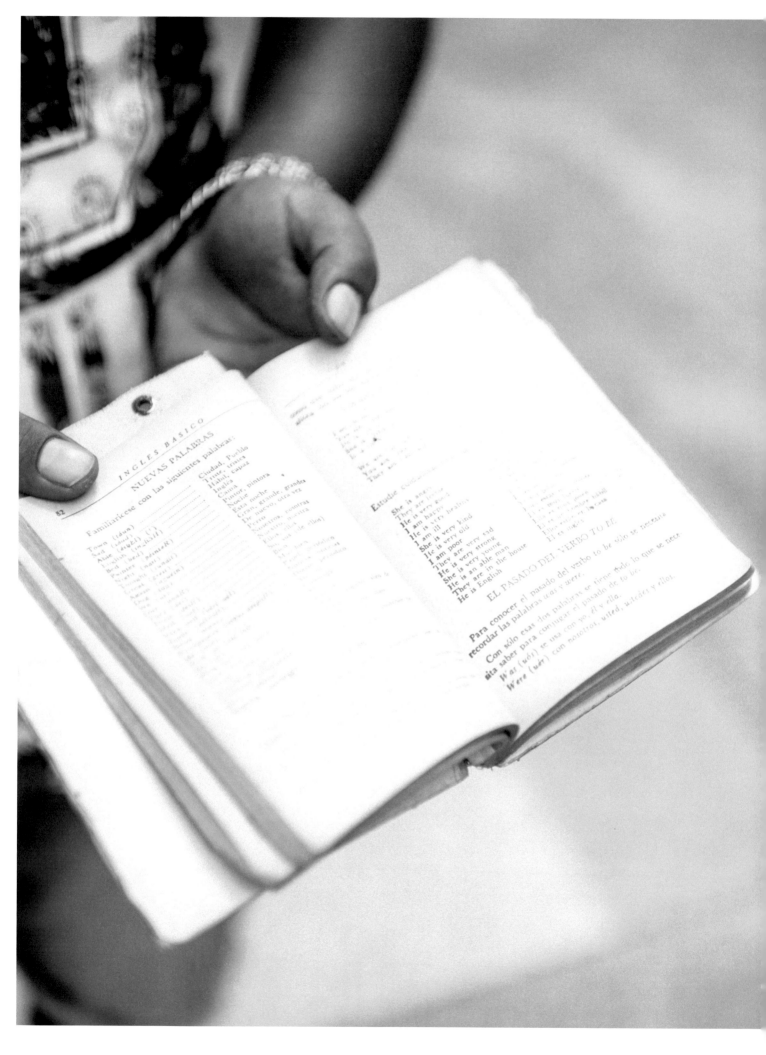

ZOE

The Zoe Kosieradzki who left Sarah Lawrence College to study abroad in Cuba is not the same as the one who came back. A girl from Minneapolis with bright eyes, a buttery voice, and big ideas about Havana, Kosieradzki now runs on strong Cuban coffee and even stronger memories of university life on the tropical island. As she remembers it, "Something happened inside of me while there that I can't let go of. It changed the way I am and see the world."

Since returning in May, Kosieradzki has been adjusting to life as a college senior back in Bronxville, New York. To round out her studies stateside, she's "studying Cuba every day, in class, through independent studies and on the news," she says, conflicted. Being in love can complicate things, she finds: "Right now I feel like my head and my heart are both in Havana. I am in love with Havana."

The coffee helps. Memories—of Old Havana and men on the street seated in tiny chairs, guarding big thermoses, and selling one-peso *tazas* of coffee—soothe her. "Now, here in New York, I drink espresso, or a *café Cubano*, every day in the morning, and again throughout the afternoon and night," she says. It's not the same, though. "Here in New York, there are coffee shops on every street corner and all over college campuses; it's the hip thing. In Cuba, it's not that at all, but it's equally strong, if not stronger, as a community and cultural thing."

For Kosieradzki, student life in Havana did not entail gulping coffee to punctuate quick hellos and goodbyes between classes. Explains Kosieradzki, "In Havana, you can't just throw on a pot of coffee, leave for a few minutes, come back, and it's done. You make it in a special pot and you have to watch it. It's a slower process." In her first days in Havana, that slow brewing was jarring, an ordinary grab-and-go daily routine suddenly operating at a frustrating, glacial pace with no internet to pass the time. Now, it's the new normal.

DEBORAH AND ROGER

They both have wide, illuminating smiles and stunning, fierce brown eyes. Their passion for art, travel, unexpected beauty, and each other, is all there, coexisting alongside unwavering Cuban pride. Deborah Orta-Cedeno and Roger Toledo Bueno, both former students, are also in love—with one another and with Havana, the city they call home.

What they remember of their experiences varies; they were in different schools, after all. Bueno graduated from ISA in 2011 and Orta-Cedeno from the University of Havana's Foreign Language Program in 2012.

We talk about college life, which begins with alcohol, long before we ever get to talking about coffee. "When I was at the university I don't remember any of my friends drinking a lot of coffee. Among my friends it was beer and rum," Orta-Cedeno recalls. Smiling, she is quick to clarify, "At the university we gathered to get cocktails more than coffee but we were never in a rush to get drunk."

In Cuba, the drinking age is 18, but that does not translate into an earlier-onset or wilder college party scene. It is still uncommon for students to live on campus; many live at home with their families until they graduate or marry. This could be one reason for more moderate consumption at the university. But Orta-Cedeno attributes it to the culture, one that does not breed overindulgence for the wrong reasons. Bueno nods and agrees, "In Cuba students don't drink to get wasted."

That's just among friends and on school grounds. Home is a different story entirely. Bueno explains, "In my house, everyone drinks coffee." He and his sister had their first sips as children at maybe seven or eight years-old, he recalls. "I think this is an important thing, to help children develop a taste for it. Drinking coffee in Cuba is part of the culture. It's not trendy. It's just there."

The way Orta-Cedeno sees it, it's hard to disentangle coffee from its political and economic context: "Farmers living on the countryside drink coffee all the time. Cuban people are very proud of our coffee, because it is some of the best in the world. But we don't have enough for all of the people here in Cuba." Cubans look out for one another, despite (or because of) the tough times they've endured, she says: "Our economic problems have made us very close to one another here in Cuba."

Bueno talks of his wanderlust and believes his paintings are nourished by a desire to see the world and share cross-cultural experiences through art. Inevitably, though, by the end of our time together, the conversation circles back to everyday life and his home in Cuba: "I opened my studio in Havana with a friend and the first thing I said was we need to get a proper coffee pot, so we can make espresso." ∎

THE PERFECT GAME

--

Writing by Alexandra Svokos
Photography by Adam Goldberg

Baseball is arguably Cuba's biggest sport. In the United States, its birthplace, the game is associated with blue skies, hometown pride, beer, and a lengthy seventh-inning stretch. But in Cuba, it's all about the coffee. Fans can get small cups to accompany the chips and popcorn that vendors sell throughout the game. Indeed, a significant part of going to see the sport in action is a fifth-inning stretch where one order of business must be attended to: The umpires must stop to drink hot coffee.

But not everyone gets to soak in that tradition forever. Baseball in Cuba, at least on a professional level, is threatened by players defecting to other countries, like the United States, where teams offer astronomical amounts of money for players to keep playing the sport they love. Roenis Elías defected in 2010 and made his Major League debut as a pitcher with the Seattle Mariners in 2014. He generally prefers Cuban coffee, but he doesn't regularly drink it, unless someone offers him a cup and he is in the mood for it. Back home, however, things were different.

"In Cuba, I'd have my grandma's coffee every morning for breakfast," Elías said. While opportunities opened up for the young player in Seattle, he left more than tropical weather behind. Now, even on his best days, it's hard to come by a perfect game. ∎

A COUP IN HAVANA

--

Writing by Kate Thorman
Photography by Adam Goldberg and Daniela Velasco

I arrive at a hand-pushed cake cart having rehearsed my order in beginner's Spanish, but, before I can actually speak, the mother-daughter team takes off across the street, cakes in tow. Around me, parents are grabbing children's hands, old men are picking themselves up off benches; everyone in Havana is sprinting for cover.

I understand as the first raindrops hit my face. Within seconds, I find myself jammed in a cafe's entrance with six other people, pressed between a young man with a messenger bag and a besuited man's oversized stomach.

In Cuba, a country where segregation between visitors and locals is essentially institutionalized, I've quickly discovered that this kind of unregulated contact with Cubans is both rare and highly unlikely. Police vigilantly watch for street harassers—not the kind who whistle and kiss at women, but rather the ones who might con you into giving them money for milk. (This trick, by the way, only works on the uneducated capitalist who doesn't know that free milk for babies is a subsidized perk of Castro's government.) Tourists and locals rarely even travel on the same long-distance buses. And, for Americans, U.S. government-sanctioned person-to-person tours—intended to give visitors a cultural perspective rather than a beach trip—only permit visits to Cuban government-approved schools, hospitals, and restaurants.

Even just wandering through Havana's crumbling streets—my preferred method of blending in or, at least, getting a picture of daily life while traveling—Americans and other foreigners stand out. Many of Cuba's tourists come from Spanish-speaking countries. But they, too, are still held at arm's length because of the currency gulf. No matter how flawless one's Cuban accent, a foreigner will still be outed at any street cart or cafe upon offering up convertible Cuban pesos, called CUCs (pronounced "kooks"), the currency created by the Cuban government just for visitors. So segregated have CUCs been that, up until a few years ago, Cubans could be arrested for having them, putting yet another damper on interactions between locals and visitors. The real question in all of this segregation is who is being protected, and from whom.

One day, perusing the stalls at the daily used book market in the Plaza de Armas, bordered by picturesque, dilapidated colonial buildings, touristy coffeehouses, and restaurants, my travel companion and I begin chatting with a young vendor. We start by asking about the books—a mix of Cuban literary classics, works in translation, and Revolutionary hero-aggrandizing graphic novels. But the conversation rapidly turns to him asking questions about us, how we came to be in Cuba as Americans, what we think of his country so far. Exchanging a look with my friend, we realize we have found our first chance at a real conversation with a Cuban—our first chance at a Cuban friend, even—and turn the tables. A law student by night, he tells us that he taught himself English and that his father fought with Castro in the mountains. He answers all our questions, offering insightful commentary both supportive and critical of the government.

The three of us chat for a good half hour, before he spots his boss approaching across the plaza, and we quickly make a few purchases so his neglect of other customers will not be noticed. Before we can even make plans to continue the conversation over a *cafecito* at one of the city's many cafes (our treat, of course, as most Cubans can't afford them), our new friend tells us that we'll have come back to the book stall if we want to chat further. His hesitance, he explains, is a result of once having been arrested for walking down the street with an American friend, accused by overzealous police of harassing tourists. His American friend protested, but to no avail, and ultimately had to come bail him out of jail.   ▶ ▶ ▶

It is my frustration with these barriers as much as my desire for a snack that prompts me to seek out a street cart as I cross the bustling Paseo del Prado, with its steady stream of brightly colored 1950s Fords and Buicks. All day, I have picked my way around the muddy puddles that dot the unpaved streets as scenes of Havana life happened around me. I watched children playing baseball in empty lots and middle-aged men displaying their rounded guts as they chatted on neighboring benches, and wished I could involve myself in the city's daily life.

At this point, in the midst of Havana's busiest plaza, I decide to make my move, spotting the hand-pushed cart with its homemade snacks of honey-soaked cakes and deep-fried dough covered in sugar. The two proprietors—they look like mother and daughter—are casually chatting with a little boy and his father, and I move to be the next customer. But I never get my chance, as I join the prescient Habaneros in running for cover, bewildered at how they can have been a step ahead of the rain.

Under the cafe's overhang, no one speaks. No Cuban men kiss or whistle or stare or even talk to me, a break in the constant attention that comes with being a woman here. There is none of the boisterous chatter that would normally fill this cafe. We all just stand together, waiting, hoping for a break in the heat that we know will not come.

Peering through the sheets of water down the uncharacteristically empty Calle Obispo, Habana Vieja's main boulevard, I make out several other pockets like ours, where random groups of strangers huddle together. A triumphant smile forces its way onto my face. Despite the government's best efforts, here I am, sharing a sense of camaraderie with a group of Cubans— at a cafe, no less. And who knows how many other foreigners are doing the same thing in those other groups down Obispo, and elsewhere in the city? It's barely significant, but, after days of frustration, it feels like my own little coup.

In a matter of minutes, almost as suddenly as it started, the rain stops. The young man with the messenger bag leaps forward and down the street, and I step out so the besuited man can hurry off toward some meeting in one of the plaza's impressive baroque buildings. The muddy streets quickly fill up again, the sky continues to rumble, and life in Havana returns to normal.

It would be a lie to say that I had a revelatory moment crammed in that cafe doorway with a handful of locals. I learned more in the conversation with the bookseller than I did in my few minutes on that cafe's step. When we scatter, I am still wary of those who approach on the street, wanting to chat about life in the U.S. up until the moment they ask for money. Cubans can still barely afford to dine at the *paladares* (that is, privately run eateries) we visit, much less at state-run restaurants or cafes. I still cannot join in the lively conversations I witness at the cafe tables around me as I sip a coffee in a place that ought to encourage such connections.

And yet, something has happened. Frustrating and insurmountable as the institutionalized segregation has been, and will continue to be, I have spent five minutes like anyone else in Havana: ignored, anonymous, banding together with others to be simply another person hiding from the rain.

But there is also something else. That same afternoon, a few hours later, after I have finally gotten that cake and coffee, something in the growling sky out over the Malecón, the city's serpentine seafront walk, strikes me as different. Before a single drop hits me, I immediately make for an overhang where an old man looks out, judging the clouds. Seconds later, the rain begins to pelt down. ∎

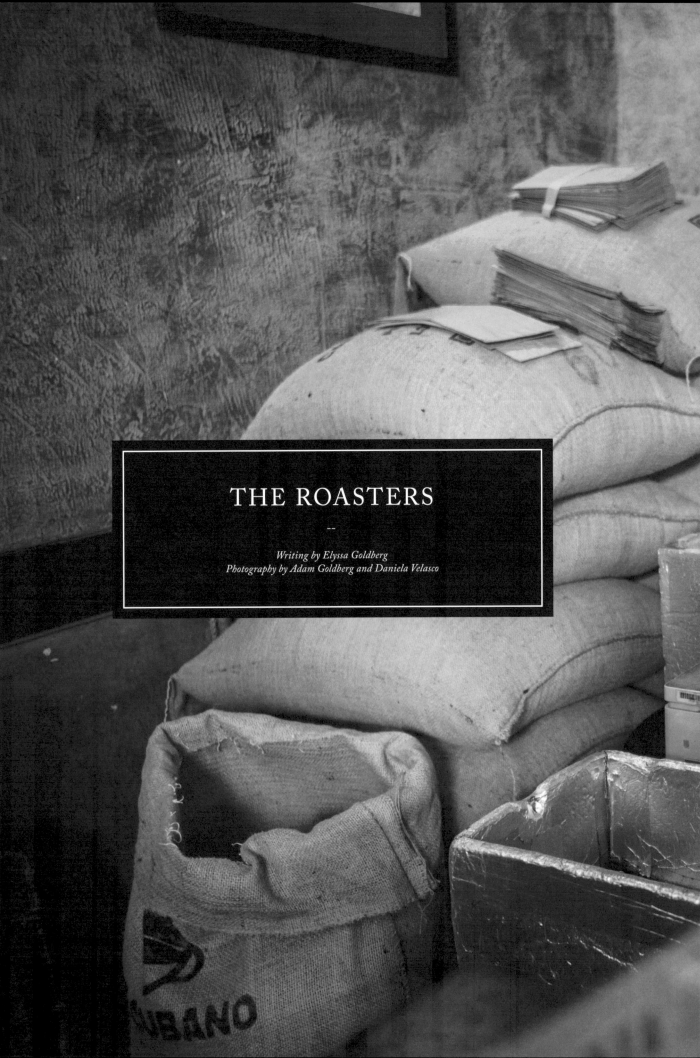

THE ROASTERS

--

Writing by Elyssa Goldberg
Photography by Adam Goldberg and Daniela Velasco

If you come to Havana looking for a well-lit microroastery and mustachioed baristas pouring latte art with laser focus, you're going to spend a long time looking. Havana has two roasteries. Both are run by the Cuban government, and neither is rigged with the gadgets and beans that have become the hallmarks of burgeoning third wave coffee culture in major cities across the globe.

Café El Escorial, the more famous of the two, opened its doors on Plaza Vieja in 2005. Located just beyond a shaded Spanish colonial-style arcade, El Escorial inhabits a storefront in the refurbished tourist center of the city—no dilapidated, collapsing buildings in eyeshot. The place is built to mirror an archetypal European cafe, the kind of cafe the government realizes is a must-have amenity for tourists.

By 9 am, there's already a line trailing out the front. The tile-covered tables on the arcade patio spill onto the plaza, and are occupied by tourists and foreigners keeping their morning routines afloat with a cup of joe that's not cut with *chícharo*. But many waiting in line are locals, who buy the coffee not for themselves (their subsidies don't cover the cost), but for foreign visitors at their *casas particulares* and tourist-frequented cafes.

No matter who's ordering, Julio is likely the one roasting. Julio moved to Havana from the countryside, where he was a mechanic, and has been roasting at El Escorial ever since. He does it by muscle memory. It helps that Julio had been roasting his whole life.

A friend, Yolanda Hernández Álvarez, explains that Cubans from *el campo* have coffee plants growing wild near their homes, a perk of inhabiting the tropical island. The plants are just part of the scenery, and it's become customary for people, like Julio, to grow up toasting the beans from those plants in large pots over open wood-burning fires in their front yards.

In Havana, Julio's job is to sustain El Escorial's bustling roasting operation, bagging (and sometimes grinding) freshly browned beans for purchase.

Café O'Reilly, located at the intersection of O'Reilly and San Ignacio, takes a different approach—a little less Europe, a little more Mall of America. The sign outside reads: "Café O'Reilly. Est. 1893," even though the waiter tells us it opened in 2014. The shop is the city's second roaster. Its polished interior gives way to walls decorated with syrupy coffee quotes from José Martí adjacent to lyrics from Cuba's de facto coffee anthem, *Ay Mama Inés*.

Like El Escorial, Café O'Reilly's menu features *cafecitos*, *cafés bombón*, and *carajillos*. Unlike El Escorial, there is no splashy view of the main square; O'Reilly's proximity to Habana Vieja's Calle Obispo is the stronger draw.

At Café O'Reilly most of the coffee-drinkers and people who buy bags of fresh-roasted coffee at O'Reilly are tourists, the staff notes. While some locals with more disposable income—from rigorous savings, or because they "*tiene FE*" (*fe* being faith, *FE* also being *familia extranjera* who send them money)—do, in fact, buy beans from O'Reilly, many also buy these beans to mix with the cheaper coffee they receive through government subsidies. "It's an economical thing," shrugs José A Salazar Martínez, the cafe's roaster.

Café El Escorial and Café O'Reilly coexist with one ultimate irony: Behind their differing veneers, both use the exact same beans and are owned by the same entity, the Cuban government. They're just branded differently, assuming the guise of capitalist competition. But the roasting method is the same at both. Yet differences remain. The fact that two different people—or more, depending on the day— are roasting the beans at the different locations means there must be some degree of variability.

As for the coffee, the beans at both are *puro*, with the distinctive dark roast astringency one grows accustomed to in the city. It's strong and sweet, with hints of chocolate and leather, the way Habaneros prefer it. Because, as Álvarez mentions, Cubans have a saying about their coffee: "*Lo tomamos muy dulce porque amarga la vida.*" We take our coffee sweet, because life is bitter.
∎

*The last names of subjects were omitted to protect their identities.

THE MYTH OF HEMINGWAY

--

Writing by Alexandra Svokos
Photography by Adam Goldberg

I have spent most of my adult travels chasing the ghost of Ernest Hemingway.

At Les Deux Magots in Paris, I sipped a *café au lait* beneath a framed black-and-white photograph of the writer, his visage looming overhead—as it does. At Bar Marsella in Barcelona, I balanced a sugar cube atop a fork that stretched across the gaping opening of a glass of absinthe. I poured water over the sugar, and watched the cube slowly dissolve, surrounded by the very same posters Ernest Hemingway looked at when he drank there. At Harry's Bar in Venice, while serving me a Bellini, a besuited waiter pointed to the exact spot Hemingway used to sit. It wasn't near mine.

Despite my devotion, I have not been to the place Papa lived for the longest: Cuba. As an American, the country had been barred from me until very recently. Up until now, the only way to know what his chosen drink tasted like and how the view from his alleged seat looked during his years in Cuba was by vivid imagination.

It doesn't help that Hemingway lived differently in Cuba than he did in the European cities that like to put his name in tour books. To spend 22 years in a place, on-and-off, you have to do more than frequent the bars and cafes.

Hemingway embedded himself into Havana in a way he did not do with other cities. He became part of the fabric of the city, disappearing into it. "Hemingway in Paris, he learned. That was a beautiful laboratory for him," said Robert Wheeler, author of *Hemingway's Paris* and the forthcoming *Hemingway's Havana*. "But in Cuba, in Havana, he lived. That was a way for him to just connect."

Hemingway set up a home outside of Havana, which he called "Finca Vigía," or the "lookout farm." He had his fishing boat, the *Pilar*, and joined the fishermen hunting the sea. He gained the fishermen's respect for his dedication to the sea, becoming like one of them. Cuban fishermen still hold admiration for Hemingway.

"His presence is very powerful, and not just in those iconic places," Wheeler said of Havana. "I felt the presence of Hemingway everywhere."

Yet when I talk to people about Hemingway, inevitably they'll bring up Paris, not Havana. I like to think this is because Hemingway was not in Havana to showboat and interact with fellow intellectuals and prove his worth. Havana is where he lived. But outside of my romantic affectations, I know, reasonably, that Hemingway is Paris because Paris is a popular Western tourist destination, accessible enough to experience and proclaim it the True Hemingway Experience on the flight home.

We think by reading his words and picking out the parts that surely must be autobiographical, we'll know him. We think by walking his path and drinking his coffee and sitting in his seat at a place he turned into an overpriced tourist destination— whether it's Les Deux Magots, El Floridita, or La Bodeguita del Medio—we'll understand him, we'll see his life, we'll finally see *him*.

But we don't really know Hemingway.

Of the books he wrote while in Cuba, including *For Whom The Bell Tolls* and *A Moveable Feast*, *The Old Man and the Sea* is the only one that took place where Hemingway lived. (*To Have and Have Not*, which he wrote mainly while living in Key West before he moved to Cuba, is also located on the island.) ▶ ▶ ▶

There is a moment in *For Whom The Bell Tolls* where Hemingway's narrator imaginatively drifts off to Cuba. In the midst of the Spanish Civil War, the main character is lying down at night and, in typical Hemingway form, his mind is racing.

"Which would you rather smell?" he asks himself before launching into a list of options. "The wind from the land as you come in toward Cuba in the dark? That was the odor of the cactus flowers, mimosa and the sea-grape shrubs. Or would you rather smell frying bacon in the morning when you are hungry? Or coffee in the morning?"

The Old Man and the Sea begins in the morning, with a boy helping the titular old man prepare for a day fishing out at sea. They put gear in the boat, then stop to share coffee. The coffee they drink is from a fishermen's store and comes in condensed milk cans.

"The old man drank his coffee slowly. It was all he would have all day and he knew that he should take it," Hemingway writes. "For a long time now eating had bored him and he never carried a lunch."

This is the image I have of Hemingway in Cuba. A man, believing himself to be old, watching the sun rise over the sea as he drinks simple coffee. "That's a very romantic image," Wheeler told me, "the sun rises and Hemingway's there and he's got a nice cup of coffee with him and he's made it from scratch."

I don't know the color of the sea, how the sand feels, how it all smells, or what the path from Finca Vigía to the bay looks like. But I can't get this image out of my head.

Ultimately there is no indication that the book is autobiographical, but I convince myself that I know what he must have been thinking, where he must have been sitting, and what it was like when he must have been drinking coffee from a condensed milk can. So, I can imagine him and where he lived from afar, in a setting completely apart from his reality, but Hemingway couldn't possibly have had an equally lively imagination, right?

Regardless of the facts, until you spend time in a place, or with a person, all you know is caricature. Take this image: Havana is Communism, dancing, and a broken economy. Or try this one: Hemingway is definitive proclamations, big game hunting, and depression.

As evidenced by the black-and-white framed portrait of Hemingway on the wall of the cafe Deux Magots in Paris, I was not the only one who longed to visualize Hemingway's life and understand how he lived it. But Hemingway, as we ghost-chasers know him, is ultimately a made-up character with the voice of a declamatory (well, unless his mind is racing in the dead of night) narrator.

It didn't stop me from wanting to experience Paris as Hemingway saw it, walking from where his house stood, near the Luxembourg Garden, to Gertrude Stein's flat and ending at the Deux Magots. It didn't stop me from downing *café au lait* after *café au lait*, writing in a notebook, and knocking into the walls as I walked downstairs to the bathrooms, imagining I was big, burly, masculine, and drunk.

I'm never going to really know Hemingway. But, at least now, I can know Havana. ∎

UNDER REPAIR

--

Photo essay by
Adam Goldberg and Daniela Velasco

The sounds of jangling recyclables, rattling tailpipes, and cranking wrenches reverberate throughout Havana. Next to well-preserved Art Deco and Baroque-style buildings languish crumbled ruins. Next to lush, overgrown weeds just outside the city are remnants of coffee plantations long gone. And beleaguered espresso machines from the 1950s soldier on, while antique Chevys skirt the city's curbs, despite missing parts. Havana is a city in constant repair. Making do is its guiding ethos, and welding together scraps finishes limited means with renewed life and beauty.

DIRTY HAVANA

--

Writing by Andrew Cole
Photography by Daniela Velasco

"I put the coffee on the burner. The sun was rising and I went to the window. From up here it's nice to see how the sun rises over the sea. Looking to eternity is a good way to not smell the ripe sleaze."

That's your welcome to Pedro Juan Gutiérrez's Havana.

Compare Gutiérrez to a Charles Bukowski or Henry Miller—he's particularly indecent and unashamed of his filth, even poetic about it. His contemporary reception in Cuba is about the same as Bukowski's or Miller's in the U.S. as well. He is rarely read there. His *oeuvre* tacks from uproarious, funny sex stories to gut-wrenching insights into the difficulties and injustices of daily life in Cuba—both themes that run afoul of Cuban censorship.

But it's the author's trilogy *Dirty Havana* that gives readers unfamiliar access to the Cuban capital. It takes place in the Special Period in Time of Peace, a euphemistically named period of widespread shortages and economic inactivity that followed the collapse of the Soviet Union, when Cuba lost its best political patron. Pedro Juan wanders aimlessly through the city, taking any opportunity he can to survive beyond the pitiful rations the government provided at the time—never more than 10 days' worth of food in a month. Hustling was a part of everyday life, for internationally acclaimed authors and street thugs alike. Dirty Havana, as Pedro Juan, the thinly veiled alter ego of the author, tells it, is a city where locals will do anything to survive.

Dysfunction during the Special Period spread to the coffee industry. At peak production in 1962, the country yielded a record 316 pounds of coffee per acre; by the 1990s, production had fallen by more than half, to just 135 pounds per acre. Levels of domestic coffee consumption still reflect the downturn experienced during the Special Period. Today, per capita coffee consumption is a quarter of 1950s levels.

As a result, coffee drinking, rather than a fascination of millennials, as it is in the States, remains "more of a tradition of the grandparents' generation," according to Michael Maisel, an associate at Engage Cuba, a civil society organization that focuses on forging ties between multinational companies and Cuba. Stove-top percolators, which can be equated to socialist Bialettis, are *de rigeur* in most Cuban homes, but you're less likely to enjoy a cup with a member of Havana's burgeoning hipster class than with their *abuela*.

Despite the pedigree of Cuban coffee, what *la abuela* is drinking isn't Ethiopian Yirgacheffe made on a La Marzocco. I know because I've sipped on their Hola! brand coffee, the kind made available in *libreta* ration shops in Havana. There's a reason that the standard *café Cubano* is heavy on sugar. The grounds themselves are unusually course—almost pebbly—and when prepared the traditional way in a percolator, the odor escapes with fury. As for the taste, it's not subtle. It's very, very darkly roasted.

In much the same way that the *Dirty Havana* trilogy replaces the reader's picture of Havana's picturesque old buildings and vivacious old women smoking cigars with a grittier one, Hola! replaces the fantasy of Cuban coffee with a glimpse into the

daily life of hardy Havana residents. This new alternative may be uglier, but it's far more interesting.

Though, that may not be the case for long. Maisel says that third wave coffee culture could be coming to Havana soon, and it could be millennials leading the charge. Under Raúl Castro, Cuba is slowly liberalizing its economy by allowing certain professions to try their hand in the private sector. The myriad professions that made the list include wicker furniture repair, pet breeding, bookbinding—and selling and roasting coffee.

This boon's not only expected for Havana's coffee culture, but also for Cuba's depressed coffee exports. "The U.S. allows the importation of certain products from Cuba if the producers are a part of a worker-run cooperative" of the sort allowed under Cuban economic law, says Jeff Siegel, Managing Editor at Green Chip Stocks, an alternative investment publication.

Sensing demand, cooperatives of coffee growers are beginning to emerge. "Organic, sustainably-grown coffee could fetch top dollar in the U.S., where most specialty coffee drinkers have never had a real cup of Cuban Coffee," says Siegel. "I think this is where these types of cooperatives could be very successful." What Maisel predicts is this: When the cooperatives take off, "a savvy Cuban will open up a *paladar*," or private restaurant, of the kind that are sprouting in many living rooms throughout the city—except this new movement will be "dedicated to coffee."

The road from a plantation in the Sierra Maestra to a morning mug abroad is still a long one, though. "Getting a read on what the [U.S.] State Department will or won't allow to be imported from Cuba is still a bit unclear, says Siegel. First impressions will be important, as well. "Specialty coffee drinkers in the U.S. are not a forgiving bunch, and if you do them wrong, they won't come back," Siegel adds. "That means providing quality and consistency is non-negotiable." Because if Americans' first experience of Cuban coffee is Hola!, they'll be saying *adiós*.

Underlying Gutiérrez' grim accounts of hunger and poverty, there's an acceptance of the present and an undying expectation that there is opportunity around the corner. Despite all evidence to the contrary, he knows he'll make it to the end of another day, where an iced rum and a beautiful woman will be waiting for him at home.

In one story, after a night out, Pedro Juan wakes up, bloodied and bruised on the Malecón, the famous seaside boulevard in downtown Havana. He's been robbed of the three dollars—a relative fortune in a city strapped for change—in his pocket. As he wanders the streets, still drunk, he says to himself, "Quit being weak. Toughen up. Toughen up, put yourself in front of the bull, grab it by the horns, and don't let it knock you down. You beat it, you throw it to the side, and you go on happy. Until the next bull comes and tries to topple you and you have to toughen up again *and you topple the bull*. That's the way it is. There's always another bull to knock down."

That was true of Havana in the Special Period, a city kept alive by roughly two million people searching for *una manera de gozar*—a way to enjoy life—amid ruins. But contemporary coffee culture in Cuba, despite its many bruises, shows the same gumption. All it needs is a shot. ∎

TODO ES LO MISMO

--

Writing by Jeva Lange
Photography by Daniela Velasco

1. Don't think of Cuba.
I can't stop thinking about it: the beach, the waves, the sugar cane, the revolution, the flag I sometimes confuse with Puerto Rico's. The high school exam I once took on the Cold War, where I had to memorize the year of the Cuban Missile Crisis and define Autarky and explain what happened at the Bay of Pigs. The final lines I sort of remember from *The Old Man and the Sea.* It's all there, stored somewhere upstairs.

2. A confession.
I have never been to Cuba but I came *this close* to a Cuban cigar when a boy showed me one at a high school dance; I almost smoked it with him but he left with another girl before we could. Another time, I came *this close* to Cuban coffee but of course it wasn't really from Cuba and there was no *espumita* to make it sweet, no rum to put in it in the morning the way they do in Havana, the way my cousin does now that he's back from studying abroad—a loophole in the United States' travel restrictions.

Instead, I've always longed from afar, trying to get as close as I can to Cuba by watching the American flag rise over the U.S. embassy in Havana, reading more Hemingway, or playing *Memorias del Subdesarrollo* (*Memories of Underdevelopment*) on loop. I can't get the city—or at least what I imagine it to be—out of my head.

3. Memorias.
Tomás Gutiérrez Alea was 40 when he directed *Memorias del Subdesarrollo*, less than a decade after the Bay of Pigs in 1961 and the Cuban Missile Crisis in 1962. Raised in an affluent family, Gutiérrez Alea nonetheless stayed in Havana after the revolution. His work, and *Memorias* in particular, looks European in that it recalls Italian neorealism, with on-location shooting intercut with documentary footage. But Gutiérrez Alea is something all his own, a filmmaker who vowed his films would never echo whatever neocolonialism was nurtured in Hollywood and Western Europe.

It was 1968 when *Memorias* was made, but in the movie, it is 1961, and everyone who can leave Havana is doing so. Sergio is a bourgeois, foreign-educated writer who expresses little regret for the dissolution of his marriage; his wife was sent away to Miami, and he has no intention of joining her abroad. In his Havana apartment, where he can look down on the city, Sergio listens repeatedly and fiendishly to an argument with her that he secretly recorded. "I am 39 years old and already an old man," he laments in the voice-over. "I feel stupid. More rotten than mature."

It's hard to tell what is real and what is fantasy in *Memorias del Subdesarrollo*, in part because Sergio is an unreliable narrator whose interpretations of events are contradicted by what the people around him say or do; in part because it is sometimes documentary and sometimes fiction; in part because you can never quite decipher whose side Gutiérrez Alea is on; and in part because of the tricky implication of that title—*Memorias*, untrustworthy as memories are. Distinguishing fiction from reality is also hard for another reason: I may drag my feet to admit it, but it's hard to tell what is real in *Memorias*, in part, because I have never been to Cuba.

When I turn on Gutiérrez Alea's film, I sympathize with Sergio: I feel stupid, more rotten than mature, casting my skewed perspective onto the screen. I make myself coffee—single-origin, from Brazil, and in a fancy automatic Bonavita coffee maker, not a no-frills French press like the one Sergio uses. I don't have a balcony, the way so many do in Havana, so I turn on my laptop, search "Havana balconies," and drink my coffee black instead.

I email my cousin. Later, he responds.

4. To: Jeva Lange
From: Hunter Marshall
Fri, Aug 7, 2015 at 9:32 PM
Subject: Coffee!
▶ ▶ ▶

Hey!

I am going to write an email rather than a text in response to your coffee query. I have a few memories about coffee in Cuba, but perhaps the most interesting (to me anyways) was this. There was a little "movie theatre" (I put it in quotes as it was simply a small patio area outside of an art gallery where they'd project images onto a white stucco wall) that showed a different film each week. It ran the gamut from The South Park Movie to more independent films. One week they were screening Jim Jarmusch's Coffee and Cigarettes and my Cuban film professor was all about Jim Jarmusch, so a bunch of us went. They brought out a bunch of small tables with checkered tablecloths (as in the movie, from the "Renee" vignette) for seating rather than more traditional theatre-style all facing the screen seating arrangement. Perhaps my favorite part of the night was that they set up a little stand where they only sold coffee and cigarettes. The cups were all quite small and porcelain (similar to the picture attached, which is from Cuba, the spoon in the picture was a personal reminder of the copious amounts of sugar added to coffee). I can't comment on whether this was reflective of the larger Cuban coffee-drinking culture, but the cups were always quite petite. There was never any 16-ounce type thing. Anyways, we all sat around watching Coffee and Cigarettes while drinking coffee and smoking cigarettes. It was quite lovely.

His email to me is a treat, as sweet as *azúcar*: just as foreign, just as grainy, with just a hint of bitterness that lingers behind my teeth.

5. The whole truth.

In *Memorias*, Sergio drinks coffee—a lot of coffee. Early on, he returns to the apartment where he once lived with his wife, takes off his shoes, writes a line on his typewriter, silently butters a slice of bread with one hand, and then picks up his drink with the other. Cigarette tucked between two fingers, he takes a sip and sets the cup back down. It is tiny; I think immediately of my cousin's email.

The wall behind Sergio is blank. The table is out of sight, too low for the camera. With the exception of an outlet behind him on the wall, Sergio is visually alone. "*Everything is the same,*" Sergio narrates moments later.

He is bored of the beaches, the cars, the lazy, eternal summer of the Caribbean, the beautiful women he runs into in every scene—Naomi, his "thin as a *Vogue* model" housecleaner, and Elena, 16, an aspiring actress.

The truths in *Memorias* are obscured through layers of perception and memory, leaving room for me to read into it what I want. Only slowly do I come to recognize that Sergio's boredom is with a world that I want to believe in but that does not—that cannot—exist.

6. What do I know?

In the end, all I can really know is Sergio. *Memorias* is reality melded with fantasy, a handful of daydreams over a cup of coffee stirred in with Gutiérrez Alea's documentary footage of starving children, revolutionaries, the burning of Havana ("*to think they once called her the Paris of the Caribbean*"), prisoners with their hands on their heads, and a speech by John F. Kennedy where the radio crackles with the words, "*…capable of striking most of the major cities in the Western hemisphere, ranging as far north as Hudson Bay, Canada, and as far south as Lima, Peru…*"

Havana is only 90 or so miles away from everything I have ever known, but I know nothing about it. Everything is a fantasy: that beach, those waves, that sugar cane, that Cuban Revolution. Hemingway, too, of course; and, yes, even Gutiérrez Alea, who shows a city constructed of Sergio's riddles and dreams. Sometimes I don't think I can even trust my cousin's *memorias*—memories he wrote out for me about a romantic evening under the stars with coffee and cigarettes in a world that no longer exists and maybe never did.

There is another version of Cuba in the stitches of documentary footage included in *Memorias del Subdesarrollo*, a Havana without coffee or cigarettes or cigars. A dance on a sidewalk interrupted by gunfire. Hunger, referenced in passing, and quickly forgotten. The director's eye, which lingers on Sergio's German girlfriend, the French press—anything foreign. Because, what's foreign is superior in Sergio's eyes.

Cuba, as I know it, is a fantasy. It's shared separately by Sergio and me, but even that I can't swallow easily anymore.

7. I changed my mind.

The last swig of coffee in Cuba is always the sweetest, the heaviest, with sugar settled at the bottom. But I live in New York City, just over one thousand miles from Havana. It would take only three hours by plane to make it to Havana; commercial airlines now fly there nonstop.

This time, as I get a mug down off the shelf, I pour my coffee and stop myself from adding another spoonful of sugar. This one I drink black.

"It wasn't like I thought it would be," Sergio says in the movie. "It's nothing." ■

CAFE BUSTELO

--

Writing by John Surico
Photography by Adam Goldberg

Next to Folgers and Maxwell House, a bright yellow brick or can of Café Bustelo's vacuum-packed coffee lights up the shelves at convenience stores and supermarkets across the United States. Maybe it's because of the price tag: there's a very good chance it will cost you less than five dollars. Or perhaps it's because it's the most exotic and colorful, by far, of the name brands Americans recognize. More likely it's the fact that, unbeknownst to many Americans, it's the closest thing they'll taste to true, Cuban coffee.

"Our generation has a frustration with anything that's mass produced," said Julia Berick, the marketing coordinator at the Tenement Museum, which features exhibits on immigrants who have passed through Manhattan's Lower East Side. The way she sees it, Bustelo's tremendous popularity has everything to do with its claim to the so near, yet so far island and the people who left it for New York. "There's something nice about it being made by someone's great-great-grandfather in the Bronx."

It's supposed to feel like family on purpose. Bustelo's website reads, "It all started when Gregorio Bustelo, a young man from Galicia, Spain, arrived in Cuba and fell in love with the coffee of the island." He fell in love with a Cuban woman, too. They married, and he became a roaster. Shortly after, the couple moved to Puerto Rico and brought their coffee-roasting operation with them. Eventually, they gained American citizenship, and joined a path many Latinos would later follow: They headed to New York.

At the turn of the twentieth century East Harlem's El Barrio looked a lot like what it does today: a hotbed of Latin American immigration in the heart of Manhattan, where Dominicans, Puerto Ricans, and Cubans seek new lives. Their countries' flags still wave from fire escapes. The smell of *empanadas* and *mofongo* waft through subway grates. And a *café con leche* or a *cortado* is almost always within reach.

In other words, Bustelo was right at home.

After spending their life savings on a roaster, Bustelo and his wife began selling coffee from their home—a practice commonplace in Cuba, even today. Bustelo went door-to-door at restaurants along Manhattan's busy streets, promoting his Cuban-style espresso. He even had a strategic schedule for roasting. "Because they lived close to a theater, they would roast coffee around the times movies would let out, so the wonderful and captivating aroma would greet people exiting the theater," the roaster's website says.

In 1931, Bustelo Coffee Roasters opened its first wholesale and commercial coffee shop on Fifth Avenue between 113th and 114th Streets, with its operations soon expanding up to the Bronx. And from there, it spread throughout New York and across the country, satisfying the caffeine-hungry Latin American immigrants entering America in large waves, searching for anything that reminded them of home.

By 2000, the Bustelo brand was bought up by Rowland Coffee Roasters, another family-owned business run by the Souto clan, who had been exiled from Cuba in 1960 when Castro took over. The name didn't change, but the location of Café Bustelo's headquarters did, relocating to America's Cuban-American stronghold, Miami. Yet its original New York flair is still well-represented on the back of every package, and now on t-shirts: "I <3 Bustelo," a shoutout to the iconic "I <3 NY" logo.

Under new management, the Souto sons—José Enrique, José Alberto, and Angel— spent the next decade glossing up and greatly expanding the Café Bustelo brand. New drinks, like Bustelo Cool (an iced-coffee version of the drink) and Dirty Bustelos (a coffee-vodka cocktail) began to appear at hip, huge events, from Coachella to Winter Music Conference, Lollapalooza, and the MTV Video Music Awards. The Café Bustelo flagship store soon opened in the lobby of the Gansevoort Hotel in Miami, and even Jennifer Lopez began sponsoring the brand on her tours. A *New York Times* headline from 2009 captured this newfound fame perfectly: "Out of the Bodega, Onto the Scene."

But with popularity came more attention and outside forces threatening to further distance the brand from its roots. In 2011, the J.M. Smucker Company acquired Rowland Coffee Roaster, taking Café Bustelo, along with other well-known Hispanic brands, like Cafe Pilon and Medaglia d'Oro. By doing so, the food giant cornered the Latin coffee market in New York,

▶ ▶ ▶

CAFÉ BUSTELO®

Café Espresso Molido • Espresso Ground Coffee ⓤ

PESO NETO 10 OZ (283g)   NET WT 10 OZ (283g)

CAFÉ BUSTELO®

Café Espresso Molido • Espresso Ground Coffee ⓤ

PESO NETO 10 OZ (283g)   NET WT 10 OZ (283g)

CAFÉ BUSTELO®

Café Espresso Molido • Espresso Ground Coffee ⓤ

PESO NETO 10 OZ (283g)   NET WT 10 OZ (283g)

southern Florida, and everywhere in between, adding the companies to a list that already included Folgers. The Soutos were pushed out of the picture.

Nearly 80 years after its humble beginnings, Café Bustelo is now fully corporatized, though nothing has changed about the coffee itself. What's more telling is who's actually drinking the coffee. Or, more significantly, who's not.

On the Tenement Museum's website, Berick has written about Bustelo as a major linchpin of Cuban-American immigration. To her, its advent and popularity is reminiscent of Russ & Daughters, a Jewish-American appetizing shop up the block that is famous for having introduced exceptional lox and whitefish to Manhattan. At first, New Yorkers didn't have the palate for all that salt. The same, she said, goes for strong espresso.

"Most mainstream Americans' tastes don't accept these things, but immigrants force them to," she noted over drip coffee at El Rey, a Latin-American luncheonette in Manhattan's Lower East Side. "But who does Café Bustelo now appeal to? More third-wave coffee drinkers. They like it because of its authenticity — it's cheap, *and* good. That's why J.M. Smucker bought it: to connect with that market."

"But the question is," she pondered out loud, "Who's going to drink it next?"

I asked Dr. Andy S. Gomez, the former Senior Fellow at the University of Miami's Institute for Cuban and Cuban-American Studies. Gomez was born in Cuba in July of 1954, just a year after Castro took power, and his family left for southern Florida in 1961, where he's lived ever since. He has only returned to his homeland three times.

For early Cuban-Americans of the 1950s and 60s, Gomez explained, drinking coffee was a staple of their Americanization. Particularly because of one small difference: there wasn't any Cuban espresso to call their own

Castro's takeover put a dead stop on coffee exports from the island of Cuba to America, amongst, of course, many other things—a regulation that is still very much in place today. So, the exiled population was forced to make do with American coffee, whether that meant using less water or more coffee in the pot. Anything that could make the coffee taste like home again.

"In the beginning, the complaint I heard all the time was American coffee was just water," Gomez recounted. "I know that when Cubans started drinking American coffee, they wished the American coffee came a little bit stronger. You know what I mean? With American coffee, you could see through the cup."

Over time, small cafes popped up around Little Havana in Miami, serving replica cafecitos, while Cuban coffee makers soon became staples of Cuban-American households, Gomez recounted. But the coffee itself was not from Cuba: with the embargo in place, other countries sold their beans off as being Cuban, and U.S. companies marketed them as such.

So, in reality, you had Bustelo, which actually roasted beans from Puerto Rico, not Cuba. And to think: one of the most prominent purveyors of Cuban espresso in America was not actually using Cuban beans.

"The older generation will still tell you that it tastes different," Gomez said. "But I think that's still part of them grasping at the days that they lived in Cuba."

"I think [Cuban coffee] is old-fashioned: it represents the old Cuba," he continued. "And we still try to grasp onto the past…a bit of our culture, our history. Our parents, our grandparents, and our great-grandparents."

That is why, over time, he explained, most Cuban-American homes began to drink more American coffee than Cuban coffee—it's a sign of assimilation, albeit enforced. And it also explains why a place like Cafe Versailles, a famous spot for Cuban lookalike coffee in Miami, is now filled with more American tourists than Cuban-Americans, and why Café Bustelo came out with an iced coffee version of their brand—simply to adapt to the times. The new generation has taken over.

Americans are clamoring to try Cuban coffee and younger Cuban-Americans are heading to Starbucks to try iced coffee or lattes—a reverse cultural exchange. A full Americanization process is at play here, and this is particularly important, Gomez noted, because of coffee's role in Cuban culture.
In short: coffee is at the center of it.

"I think the best way I can put it to you is that drinking Cuban coffee has always been an opportunity in public, or even at home, to discuss politics. They go hand in hand, no matter what side of the aisle you're on," Gomez told me. "We love to talk about issues with a good cup of Cuban coffee in our hands."

"Sometimes two, sometimes three," he continued, "depending on how hot the topic is. It gets our blood boiling."

So, just as the younger generation's taste buds have cooled to Cuban coffee, so, too, have their worldviews in changing times. While the older generation of Cuban-Americans has been characterized as conservative towards its homeland, the youth, Gomez said, might be taking a different stance.

"When she came to interview me, a friend of mine said that she had a hard time at Cafe Versailles finding people of the younger generation that were against the Obama administration's policies towards Cuba," he added. "Or simply even cared."

"We have gone from a politics of passion to a politics of realism," he continued.

Although the Cuban-American population is, on average, older than other foreign-born ethnic groups in America, most of the 1.1 million Cuban-Americans here, he added, were born after the revolution, and a growing portion of them within the past two decades. The attachment to the old Cuba — or the old Cuban coffee — is a tale their grandparents have told them with wide eyes. It is a main part of a culture that they're very much not a part of.

And that, Gomez said, is how Americanization works: "What we're doing more now is building bridges with the Cuban people," he added.

Still, Café Bustelo — this cross of so many things: immigration, assimilation, *caffeine* — has a purpose. It brings non-Cuban Americans into the fold, and permits them to enjoy a past that Gomez's generation remembers. It also serves as a souvenir of what Gomez calls the Cuban mystique; one that holds a "very rich culture and history, but is at the same time, very complicated," he said, more seriously. "I've described it as a badly written Shakespearean play with no ending."

He paused, then said, "John, I'm still looking for the ending." ∎

INTANGIBLE EXPORTS

--

Writing by Rachel Eva Lim
Photography by Daniela Velasco

In Colorado's land-locked capital, surrounded by towering mountains and evergreens, Emmett Barr whips up a *café con leche* at Buchi Café Cubano—no palm trees in sight. The United States is just 90 miles from Cuban shores, but it can seem a world away. It's why he and other cafe owners are attempting to recreate the Havana coffee-drinking experience stateside. Some of these cafes, including Cuban Coffee Queen and 5 Brothers in Key West and Versailles and Islas Canarias in Miami, are clustered in Florida, where there is a large Cuban population. Others, like Buchi Café Cubano, have opened outside of the gravitational pull of Havana's geographic and cultural influence.

Because, when it comes to emulating Cuban coffee culture, there only seem to be three non-negotiable rules. First, the coffee must be strong and sweet; in Havana, it's laced with raw sugar during the brewing process and there's less milk than what most Americans are used to. Second, it must be taken liberally. Then, above all else, it must be enjoyed in good company. Coffee in Havana is an intensely social activity, cherished as both a social lubricant and sign of hospitality. Havana residents adopt a decidedly unhurried approach to partaking in their coffee, and view it as an opportunity to slow down and bring people together.

"You start brewing a *café Cubano* the second a guest steps into your home, no questions asked," says Vivian Hernández-Jackson, who runs Azúcar, a Cuban cafe in San Diego. Being raised by Cuban parents who were exiled by Castro's government as teenagers exposed her to coffee from a young age. "I was drinking a straight *café con leche* by the time I was 12." Living in a coffee-obsessed city like Miami also helped. "Cuban coffee is as important to Miami as flamingos, Gloria Estefan, and Miami Vice," Hernández-Jackson quips. "I don't know any Cubans in Miami who are tea drinkers, unless they're sick or trying to go to sleep."

Hernández-Jackson's menu includes all the standard drinks you'd find at a traditional cafe in Havana. She even gets her coffee beans from Gaviña—a family friend's company that originated in Cuba in 1870 and moved its operations to California in 1967. "They source their beans from all over the world and I feel that the Old Havana-style roast is what makes the coffee authentic, not the provenance of the beans themselves," Hernández-Jackson says. She follows the traditional method of adding Demerara sugar during the espresso brewing process rather than after. This allows the sucrose to hydrolyze via the heat from the espresso and render a smoother, thicker brew with a unique layer of sweet *crema* on top.

Then there's Jeremy Sapienza, who co-founded Cafetería La Mejor in Brooklyn with his partner Luis Velázquez. While Sapienza has no familial connection to Cuba, his attraction to Havana's coffee culture was developed over the course of his upbringing. The Miami native grew up patronizing the many Cuban restaurants and cafes that dot the city's landscape—a result of around 1.2 million Cuban immigrants arriving in the Greater Miami area over the past six decades. "There are $5,000 espresso machines in pretty much every gas station, lunch counter, deli, and supermarket in Miami, which is pretty wild," Sapienza notes. For the first several years that Sapienza and Velázquez lived in New York, they lamented the lack of local cafes serving quality Cuban coffee. All they wanted was a little taste of home; so, they opened Cafetería La Mejor. "There were some of the old standards in Manhattan but they are honestly terrible," Sapienza says. "I thought an updated 'Brooklynized' twist on a Floridian classic would be a cool idea."

While brewing methods and reverence for coffee-drinking is easily exported, some aspects of Cuban coffee culture remain firmly on the island. For instance, none of the Cuban cafes in the U.S. are subject to the same government rations as Havana residents, which means they don't have to stretch coffee with *chícharo*.

In fact, Sapienza is proud of the differences, and is quick to stress that his cafe embodies a more distinctly Floridian, even if by way of Havana, coffee experience. "I've tried to make it clear that Cafetería La Mejor is Floridian, but it's hard because we serve Cuban coffee and a sandwich—invented in Florida—called a Cuban sandwich," Sapienza says. Yet, he also raises the question of whether the missing Cuban connection should have any bearing on the authenticity of his business. "It's like an Irish New Yorker moving to Idaho and opening a New York-style pizza place," Sapienza suggests. "Is he Italian? Does it matter?"   ▶ ▶ ▶

Marius Venter, the owner of Key West's Cuban Coffee Queen, Hernández-Jackson, and Sapienza are all firm in their commitment to transmit an authentic Havana cafe experience to their customers. But first they have to meet American palates halfway—somewhere between third wave cafe culture and old-fashioned tradition. Says Sapienza of his adherence to third wave coffee practices, "We may toss sugar, salt, and butter in the *café con leche*, but we still dial in and make sure we're following the rules that we know will make the coffee taste its best." In Cafetería La Mejor's case, this entails using top-shelf ingredients: Stumptown Coffee Roasters beans, Hudson Valley milk, and upstate New York pasture-raised pork for sandwiches. It also means finishing off drinks with latte art and silky microfoam, perfected over countless hours of training. Azúcar offers patrons the option of adding soy, almond, or coconut milk to their Cuban coffee, and many of its drinks also come in iced versions to cater to customers' requests.

But Sapienza doesn't think that this makes his coffee any less *a lo Cubano* at heart. "We also put two sugars in every coffee and that's just how it's gonna be unless customers ask otherwise," Sapienza says.

Venter adopts similar principles, taking pride in the extra flair he adds to standard Cuban recipes. "We put a little spin on things such as serving a regular Americano with a shot of *café Cubano* or doing an iced *café con leche* with espresso ice cubes, but on the whole we're definitely trying to stay true to the Cuban experience."

Indeed, while they're happy to embrace preparations they've picked up from Cuban coffee culture, and perhaps improve on them, none are willing to compromise on quality, taste, or social responsibility in order to claim some version of authenticity. "They use shit ingredients at most 'authentic' places, and that's not something I'm willing to do for authenticity's sake," Sapienza asserts. "The culture has to necessarily serve as inspiration, and since we've ripped it out of its native context we've had to adapt it to local conditions."

Venter adopts a similar mindset, and has made some deliberate modifications to the traditional way of doing things. Cuban Coffee Queen serves its drinks and sandwiches in biodegradable paper containers, while many other Cuban cafes in Key West—and Havana itself—use Styrofoam or small plastic cups. "It sets us apart from other local joints, but I don't think it makes us any less credible," he argues. Such a modification helps Cuban Coffee Queen compete with other cafes in the area while staying true to its Cuban roots.

Purists may argue that these owners' modifications divorce the experience they're providing from the coffee-drinking tradition that's alive and well on the streets of Havana. But maybe that's a good thing, and it'd be hard to say that they aren't dedicated to preserving the social aspect of Cuban coffee culture. Azúcar and Cuban Coffee Queen have large seating areas for customers to linger over their drinks with friends, and Cuban Coffee Queen and Cafetería La Mejor also make use of the quintessentially Cuban window-ordering experience—the *ventanilla*—as a way for baristas to interact with customers. It may be spiffier than Havana, but what does it matter if the coffee's expertly executed and the vibe is right, they challenge.

Both Venter and Hernández-Jackson state that one of the most rewarding parts of the job is when native Cubans or Miami transplants stop by to get their Cuban coffee fix. At Cafetería La Mejor, Sapienza gets Cubans and Floridians flocking to his Bushwick cafe, driven by a sense of nostalgia. "The minute they see the bright teal façade, the pink neon, and the brass outside counter from down the block and across the street, they *know* what it is," Sapienza says. "That means I did it right." ∎

THE TASTE OF HOME

--

Writing by Elena Sheppard
Photography by Adam Goldberg

Meet me at five years old. I didn't drink coffee (it took 20 years before I could stand the taste) but I did accompany my *abuelo*, my grandfather, on walks to get his *cafecito*. On the way to the *cafetería*—the coffee shop, a coffee counter—I held his hand.

It was Miami, but it could've been Havana. *The Cubanos* designed it that way. In the afternoons on Calle Ocho, the heart of Miami's Little Havana, they stood around in their billowing *guayaberas* and wool slacks, drinking *cafecitos* passed through shop windows, threads of steam rising from their Dixie cups. They spoke Spanish, and talked politics, women, and *la patria*. And they did it all while sipping coffee that tasted like home: purse-your-lips bitter, suck-your-teeth strong, but sweet, if anyone asked. Sometimes they brought their grandchildren, like me, who spoke English before Spanish and didn't understand why a tiny cup of scalding coffee would be the right thing to drink in the summer heat. The men, they stood in clusters on the street corners and sipped while their grandchildren ate *pastelitos de guayaba* from paper bags. It was a daily matinee, a ritual, a piece of *la isla* brought to *los Estados Unidos*. Except everything—even the coffee, *viejo*—was better in Cuba. And don't you forget it.

This is how they made coffee at my house:

-Bustelo was the only brand. It was one from the yellow can.
-You would untwist the stovetop espresso maker, the *cafetera*, until the top and bottom came apart.
-Then you'd fill it with coffee, and after, fill it with water.
-Next, you would twist to seal the two halves.
-Then you would heat it on the stove until the coffee rose, and you could hear it percolating.
-We'd shout, *"Quién quiere café?" "Who wants coffee?"*
-*Cortaditos* were preferred: We would fill espresso cups with sugar, coffee, and a splash of milk—"to cut it," my mother would say.

The years passed and the temperature chilled. I'd know it was the holidays, because kids like me had Christmas radar; we can feel it coming 12 months out. I would pad down the stairs in socked feet and pause just at the spot where I could see the reflection of the Christmas tree in the living room mirror. The tree was skirted with gifts and it seemed to me that Santa Claus must have left the lights on. Outside the living room windows, the sun started to fan through the trees—not palm trees, though, because, at this point, I lived in New York.

In the kitchen, Nana filled the coffee maker. "We're the only two up, Elenita," she said, addressing me. Nana sealed the two halves of the *cafetera* and placed it on the stove.

Nana knew how to wake up a house. "We'll be as noisy as possible," she said. She clanged cups, sugar bowls, and spoons as she got the coffee ready. By the time the rest of the house was up, *café con leche* was made. I knew that there were gifts but, these days, I can't seem to remember a single one. I just remember coffee and the smell of it caught in my throat. I just remember the sound of Nana ringing spoons in cups. *Qué va.*

My father, an American, drinks Cuban coffee every morning too. But, the way he tells it, when he first met my grandparents, they were suspicious of him. He wanted the heart of their daughter, my mother, but spoke no Spanish and drank no Cuban coffee. Now, he serves his mother-in-law. They still don't share a language but they do share a pot of coffee, a *colada*. *"Café?"* he asks her. *"Sí"* she says. *"Y azúcar?"* he asks her. *"Sí,"* she says. He pours, he stirs, and he hands over the goods. *"Qué rico,"* she says, knowing that no son-in-law can be so bad who makes coffee so well.

My grandmother tells stories. "After parties we'd always stop for snacks," my grandmother says, reminding me of her upbringing. I remember her saying: "It'd be midnight, your feet would be throbbing from dancing, and we'd go for sandwiches

▶ ▶ ▶

called *medianoches* (midnight was the hour to eat them) and *cafecitos*. *Medianoches* for all, shots of liquor for some, shots of coffee for others. Then you wake up in the morning, more coffee. In the afternoon: coffee. If a friend stops by: coffee. Evening time? Coffee. With all the caffeine in us, it's a miracle the whole island didn't just up and swim to Europe."

I am now 27, in the hospital room when my grandmother wakes from surgery. It is after midnight and the room is quiet; machines buzz and liquids drip, as if to let you know that, yes, medicine is happening. My grandmother looks small, and there is writing on her legs where the surgeon had to cut. The hospital gown nearly swallows her whole; on her feet she wears hospital-administered socks. My grandmother stirs; she opens her eyes, looks up, and says, *"Y mi café?"*

I've often wondered about the things we carry with us, the stories, the people, the flavors—*los sabores*. What made it to me? What was forgotten along the way? What I do know is that, when packing for a new life, you must choose wisely what crosses the water, even when it's only 90 miles from one life to the next. Here's what came to the United States (no matter what), at least according to my grandmother:

-Two daughters, one in each hand.
-A wedding band. That can't be left behind.
-Five American dollars.
-A head full of memories: good ones to call upon in bad times, bad ones to surface in good.
-Faith.
-One suitcase packed only with the essentials.
-Two toys, one per daughter.
-A lifelong taste for Cuban food and a bevy of know-them-by-heart recipes.
-Conviction that you'll be home in no time. How long can you really be gone with milk still in the fridge?
-*Fuerza*. Strength.

One last thing: Cuban coffee, something bitter that we force so well to be sweet. ∎

UP ALL NIGHT

--

Writing by Angela Almeida and John Surico
Photography by Adam Goldberg

It's hard to see beyond the bright glare of the iPads, iPhones, and digital cameras.

Ironic, too, given the lack of internet access, and where we are: the Buena Vista Social Club, a place with "good view" in its name. But tonight, the open-air palace that has been sold to us as Fidel Castro's former home is flooded with hordes of tour groups—some 20 to 30 in size—none of which realize that the better show is beyond their glowing screens.

For years, the Buena Vista Social Club was closed. It had come to represent the Western leisure of the Batista regime—a pre-Castro fixture of the early 1950s, where foreigners could lavishly spend money—and therefore, it was effectively erased from Cuban nightlife in the early days of the revolution. But within the past two decades, as tourism has gradually returned to the country, the club has re-opened, once again offering classic Cuban music and dance to the Westerners who flock here in search of the Old Havana.

Despite the abundance of Cuba Libres and mojitos, the dance floor is empty, save for the Afro-Cuban salsa performers who wade into the crowd, making sure to always follow up their Spanish with English translations. This is a safe haven for tourists. (Even the waiters are uncharacteristically bilingual.) And for 55 CUC, or the equivalent of $55, the near-retirees, with their selfie sticks in hand, are buying what they've been sold: "*Una Noche Como Fue En Los Años 50s*," the hotel pamphlets read. "A night like it was in the Fifties."

Yet across town, in the more residential neighborhood of Vedado, a different scene is transpiring outside of a converted peanut oil factory. There, a line of Cuban teenagers wraps around a sprawling three-floor performance and art space, better known as La Fábrica de Arte Cubano (FAC). It's Saturday, so demand for entrance into the place that's been called the "future" of Cuban nightlife is high.

Espresso, cortado, Americano, cappuccino. For the Cubans crowded around the bars of late-night Havana, coffee is still very much a fixture on the menu. In fact, nestled on the second floor of La Fábrica is a full-service coffee bar that stays open all night to revelers. "It's like our Red Bull," said the bartender there, as she served a frothy pick-me-up. "People need the energy to stay out."

Downstairs, bottles of the famous rum Havana Club circle in perpetual motion overhead on an Art Deco assembly line of sorts. The bartender dishes out mojitos for 2 CUC and Cristal beers for 1—and photos of a naked man perusing through a pig-sty, a naked woman pressed between a wall, and a line of naked women's feet on the beach are free for viewing. Make it up the flight of stairs and you'll see Michael Jackson's "Bad" video, which is projected onto a cinema screen.

It's frenetic for 1am, this strange hybrid of a Brooklyn art gallery, a Berlin nightclub, and a Cuban block party. On the outdoor patio, Roberto, an older friend from Havana who accompanied us, looked out at the young people who gathered to smoke and chat the night away. "It's a different time to be a child," he said.

Started by Cuban multimedia artist, X (Equis) Alfonso, La Fábrica, in the words of its owner, is meant to be "authentic and different from the contemporary globalized currents"—a place that strives to represent a new direction for the youth of Cuba. And perhaps, it is a sign of what is to come in these changing times.

In May of 2016, the country will witness its first electronic music festival in Santiago de Cuba; branded as 'MANANA,' the music has been described as "Afro-Cuban Folkloric and Electronic." Meanwhile, after banning it from parties in 2012, the Cuban government has recently relaxed its restrictions on reggaeton, which is, by far, the most popular genre of music for the youth today. Even the space of La Fábrica itself has been leased out to X Alfonso by a government arm, the Ministry of Culture, since early 2014.

Yet one tradition of old-world Cuba lives on, even in this new world of nightlife.

When we leave, we stumble down the cobblestone *calles* at 4am, not far from the tourist-laden streets of Obispo and Mercaderes, to where Juan sits on a stool beside his first-floor window, waiting for the night dwellers to make their way home. He has a boiling pot of Café Hola ready to go, complete with six ceramic cups for cafecitos.

"Sometimes, I wake up to a knock on the door," Juan says, smiling. "*Hola! Dónde está el café?*"

For most of his life, Juan worked as a chef in restaurants throughout Cuba. However, his first foray into coffee-making didn't come until he shifted from the kitchen to the front-of-house, as a waiter at a cafe designed for tourists in Old Havana. It was there that Juan learned how to properly pack a Cuban coffee maker, or a *cafetera*. Now retired, Juan spends his days, from 4am to 11pm, sitting by his window and serving his made-for-Cuba blend—five spoonfuls of coffee, five spoonfuls of *azúcar*.

As the bars' energy dwindles, window coffee, like Juan's, cap off Havana nights. These *ventanillas*, as locals affectionately call them, provide a sweet refuge away from two worlds: one desperately nostalgic for a Cuba that once was; the other, rapidly embracing a Cuba that could be. Yet sitting in Juan's kitchen, watching him dutifully prepare his brew, somehow feels like the only constant of the night—or one of the few parts of Cuban identity that doesn't seem in flux.

"Cubans always drink coffee," Juan explains. "They drink it 24 hours a day." ∎

CHASING LIGHT

--

Writing by Elyssa Goldberg
Photography by Jason Fitz

When Toronto photographer Jason Fitz landed at José Martí International Airport, he knew he would only have five hours to spend in Havana, so he came with a game plan. "I knew what spots I wanted to hit and had those mapped out to a T," he remembers. Even still, time flies in the photogenic city, and when you're under the gun, it's a series of quick snaps punctuated by quicker sprints to the next spot, following moving people and light. There's no time for redos.

For a photographer who's seen it all, and has 64,000 followers on Instagram, Havana still took Fitz (@jasonfitzzz) by surprise. There were the things he recognized: people, moving targets with places to go and more people to meet. And there were things that confounded him with their differences: "Living in North America, it feels like there is something everywhere. Some company has taken over this corner, or occupies that building." In Cuba, where dimly lit storefronts don't scream for the attention of passersby, that is not the case.

Yet Fitz still laments his inability to get a good Cuban coffee back on Canadian soil. He loves the way his wife sneaks cinnamon into his morning home-brew, but he fell unexpectedly for the sweet *café con leche* he had every morning on the island: "I can safely say I have not enjoyed another cup of coffee as much since." That's just how it happens in Cuba. Just ask Fitz's eldest son, who also fell in love with the place. Every day, he still asks his dad, "What do you think the people are doing in Cuba right now?"

When the clock ran out, Fitz high-tailed it out of the frenetic city center and he and his family planted themselves on the pristine beaches of Varadero. Because, as Fitz remembers it, "Shooting in Havana was like no other experience I've had with my camera," and chasing light in the untiring capital is hard work. ∎

CUBA LIBRO

--

Writing by Kathryn Curto
Photography by Adam Goldberg

After over a decade of living in Havana, healthcare journalist Conner Gorry found herself staring down a bag of books that needed a home. A friend dropped them off, and said they'd go to waste if she didn't take them.

"I looked at this hefty, yellow bag of books for about six months," she says. "Then I thought, you know, now it's possible to open private businesses *and* there's a really strong coffee culture in Cuba." From that loose idea came Cuba Libro, Havana's first English bookstore and coffeehouse.

Doors to this coffee shop inside of a house on a residential corner in Havana's Vedado neighborhood opened in the summer of 2013; and in the past two years, the cafe has expanded not only its lineup of offerings (way beyond caffeinated beverages and gently used novels) but also its customer base (way beyond academic tourists and literary types). This kind of growth should come as no surprise to those who know Gorry, the cafe's resolute founder, who is determined to fill cultural gaps at her come-one-and-all establishment.

"When Conner told me about the idea of opening Cuba Libro I wondered what kind of audience it might attract. Two years later, I have to say, it's been amazing," offers Manuel Alejandro Gil, a friend of Gorry's, a Cuban software engineer who built Cuba Libro's website, and a self-proclaimed coffee addict. Gil recently left Havana for a job in Santiago de Chile, where he now lives with his family—despite the subpar coffee there. He laments, "There's nothing like Cuban coffee."

Most of the people hanging around Cuba Libro, which is laid out with three open sitting areas—a living room, an outdoor tropical patio garden, and a kitchen—are students. Gorry says most of the students aren't from the University of Havana; they're actually from the Latin American Medical School (ELAM), and she's happy to give those students whatever support she can. The idea behind ELAM is to give students six years of free medical education so that, upon graduation, many go home to low-income neighborhoods and provide essential healthcare services to underserved communities. "It works," says Gorry of the program.

The ELAM students, among others from the Instituto Superior de Artes (ISA)—"the Juilliard of art here in Havana," as Gorry describes it—treat the place like an open-door living room, a comfortable space they can hang out, read, and socialize over coffee. "People go to Cuba Libro to have some time to relax; have a coffee or other drinks; and talk or study. It is indeed a very nice and relaxed spot in the middle of Vedado, surrounded with big trees that invite you to sit and relax," Gil explains.

But, in case the English-language books didn't give it away, the cafe's not a Cuban-only institution. You're equally likely to find English-speakers as you are Spanish-speakers there. As Gorry describes it, Cubans sit out front and English speakers float around. That's how she likes it: Since so many English-speakers find it difficult to find information in Havana or ask locals questions, Gorry wanted to create a space that would facilitate such interactions. The hope is that, if people linger long enough, they may actually hang out and get to talking, maybe go out for a night on the town, or leave the cafe with some new friends in tow.

"We want to be accessible to all, to build community," Gorry notes. "Here is this society that is 90 miles away from U.S. shores that has a completely different way of organizing itself. When people come, they come with expectations, of course. But those expectations are completely skewed toward the surface, based on a shallow understanding of Cuban life. I wanted to provide a space where Cubans and foreigners could just meet naturally, make conversation, and go beyond the surface, go deeper."

In order to make that a reality, she hosts tour groups from the U.S. and elsewhere. She and her staff also partner with local schools to offer English classes. There are concerts, art openings, classes, readings and book signings at Cuba Libro. Not to mention a free condom program. (Gorry says they've given out close to 6,000 since opening.)

She also serves coffee—lots of it. Using beans from one of the city's government-run roasteries, customers choose from a *café bombón*, *cafecito*, or *café Cubano*—all prepared in the house's small kitchen. The drinks facilitate conversation and help visitors settle in. Finding comfort in coffee is part of being in Havana, and Cuba Libro is no exception.

Think of it this way: At a recent discussion on traditional Cuban dance, Benjamin Lapidus, a musician, ethnomusicologist, and author explained that coffee beans are so woven into the social fabric of the island that in the *nengón*, a dance performed in the city of Baracoa, dancers move in rhythms and patterns mimetic of spreading coffee out to dry.

It is between sips of Cuba Libro's coffee, listed on the menu in both of the country's currencies, that cultural gaps are bridged. For instance, when Gorry first assembled her small (but mighty) library, Cuban friends warned her that a lending library was out of the question. Many books were stolen from government-run lending libraries during the Special Period, they said. But she hasn't had a problem so far. Gorry revels in proving wrong naysayers who question the utility of an English-language library in the Spanish-speaking country. It helps that new legislation requires that all university students in Havana graduate speaking English, and she's got an unimposing substitute English-language living room for practice.

Gorry views Cuba Libro as a lab for new social, ethical, and environmental initiatives taking root in the city where, she says, "There are so many wonderful things coming to Havana, but most locals don't have access to them." But if this Cuban coffeehouse can be a place where friends are made, coffee is poured, and stories are exchanged, then she's done her job.

"I used to go there every week," Gil recalls. "The coffee, combined with Conner's open and easygoing personality makes the place a really refreshing experience."

Amidst hammocks, rocking chairs, and a two-seater swing, a large rainbow flag—a gift from a Cuban neighbor—sways in the Vedado garden, a sign of camaraderie brewing. Here, coffee and conversation, Spanish-speakers and English-speakers, and the present and optimistic future seem to comingle under the lush canopy shading Cuba Libro's yard. ∎

TIPPING POINT:
Q&A WITH PHILLIP OPPENHEIM

--

Interview by Sarah Kollmorgen
Photography by Adam Goldberg

Today, planning a cafe crawl through Havana might not be the best idea: Coffee shop culture, like the country's economy, has been slow to rebound to its former glory after years of economic hardship. But that will soon change if one British Cubaphile has his way.

Phillip Oppenheim, a former Treasury minister and entrepreneur from England, has been making trips to Cuba since the 1990s in order to stock up on sugar and rum for Cubana, his Cuban-themed restaurant in London. Oppenheim even boasts that Cubana introduced mojitos to the United Kingdom. It all started when, during one of his many trips to the island nation, Oppenheim happened upon a cup of authentic Cuban coffee made with beans from the island. It was in that moment that he knew he had to get involved in the Cuban coffee scene, somehow.

Sorting out the details of foreign investment in the Cuban agriculture sector was no walk in the park: It took Oppenheim seven years of meeting with Cuban farmers and government members before his brainchild, Alma de Cuba, came to fruition in 2013. Over four years, Alma de Cuba will invest around $4 million in the coffee industry for things such as equipment such as de-pulping plants, new testing laboratories, and veterinary support for mules used for transportation in the unpaved mountains. With the help of a few friends and business partners, and hopefully foreign investors down the line, Oppenheim and Alma de Cuba want more than anything to work with Cuban farmers, or *campesinos*, in the southeast region of Cuba and see the Cuban coffee industry reach new heights.

How did you get started with Alma de Cuba?
Cuba used to be a very big coffee grower. Before the revolution, it had a big position in fine coffees. It has a lot of natural advantages: the geology, the latitude, the height of the mountains, the quality of the soil, and its location in the tropics, but not too close to the equator. Coffee grown at higher altitudes develops relatively slowly; as a result, their flavors are much more subtle. So, Cuba has a lot of advantages as a coffee-growing area.

What first drew you to Cuban coffee?
I was already involved in Cuba through Cubana, a sort of restaurant-bar group in England—we were making mojitos 20 years ago and specialized in authentic Cuban food and drinks. I was involved in a small emerging-markets front for Cuba, and coffee was one of the areas we decided was ripe for investment. We got together with one of the main people in the Jamaican Blue Mountain [a classification of coffee] industry and together we worked on this project for many years with the Cubans.

Being Cuba, obviously investment is not as straightforward. But over the years we developed a strategy for concentrating in the southeast of Cuba, where the best coffee-growing region is, aiming to improve productivity, quality, and develop micro-regional coffees. We're just really at the very, very end of a long negotiating period, and the project proper begins next year [in 2016]. But we already trade quite a lot of Cuban green beans and we have our own roasted brand, which is called Alma de Cuba.

What brought you to Cuba in the first place, and what about it keeps you going back?
Well, I have a varied background as an entrepreneur setting up businesses. I'd also been a journalist. I spent a lot of time in the old Communist bloc countries, and I'd actually been to all of them, except for Cuba, funny enough. I also had a passionate interest in food and drink. One of the things I always wanted to do was set up a restaurant or bar, and when I had the opportunity to do that, I had originally hoped to do a Japanese restaurant, because I'd worked in Japan and like Japanese food. However, in the U.K. and Europe, by the mid-90s, there were a lot of Japanese restaurants, and we—the people I was working with and I—wanted to do something that felt a little more original. Cuba was suggested.

We went there and we realized there was fantastic culture, a lot of different types of dance music, and a tropical feel with cigars and cocktails. We discovered mojitos in Cuba, which weren't really known then. I'm also into Cuban food, which took a bit of discovering because after the revolution, Cuban food in Cuba had gone into decline. But after looking at old recipe books, speaking to old plantation chefs, learning recipes from the Cuban-American community, we realized Cuba has a wonderful cuisine, and would be great for the restaurant.

As I visited Cuba more often—partly to make sure we were as authentic as possible, but also partly to get things like rum, which we imported directly—I developed a great love for the country, because of its varied culture. The Spanish colonists used to stay in Cuba; whereas the British, French, and Dutch colonists used to go to the West Indies, make their money, come home and build these great buildings at home. Small farmers up through higher-ranking society people would stay and live in Cuba, bring up children in Cuba, and build beautiful cities and expanses [there]. I became very fond of Cuba and the Cuban people, culture, background, and fantastic history.

Do you still often go to Cuba?
Yes, I go about two or three times a year.

What do Cuban coffee farmers think about your work within the Cuban coffee industry?
The big coffee estates have mostly closed down, so all of the coffee we're dealing with is grown by small farmers. They tend now not to be specialists; they are mostly subsistence farmers. But the people who run the operations on the ground have a substantial coffee plant near Santiago de Cuba, where the final sorting happens. So on one hand you've got these very technocratic, very enthusiastic people, who are a little bit starved of funds and feel perhaps that they want a little bit more autonomy from the government in Havana. And up in the mountains you've got the coffee farmers with smaller operations who would very much like more investment in their industry, better prices for their coffee, those sort of things. So these groups down in the far southeast of the country—which is about 800 to 900 kilometers away from Havana—are very enthusiastic for the investment program we've got and the greater autonomy they'll get as a result of this deal from the government.

If you're passing through Havana, do you have a go-to coffee shop or drink?
I wish there was. You've got to bear in mind that Cuba has been run as a socialist country for a long time. There are some small, independent restaurants now. But, by and large, coffee-drinking-in-cafes culture hasn't really caught on there. You would think that they would be a big coffee-drinking nation—and they are to an extent. But the Cuban coffee tradition is to have a very dark roast coffee, which is not necessarily good for high-quality mountain coffees.

Can you describe what you mean by high-quality?
The first thing you need to know is that high altitude-grown coffees tend to be much subtler in flavor than industrial coffee crops grown in great big rows in places like Brazil. Those coffees are fine as general coffees, but a mountain coffee will develop more slowly, and the flavors will be better—a more subtle flavor. Our coffee grows at altitudes between 600 and 800 meters, which is somewhere in excess of 2,000 feet. Now that's not super-high grown coffee—you know, not the rarefied super-premium coffee. But for a general coffee it's [grown] pretty high.

You would not want to high-roast these coffees. Some people equate dark coffee with good coffee—it's not, it's just over-roasted to hide the imperfections. A medium-high roast is always nicer than a high-roasted if it's a good coffee. If you took our coffee and you gave it a medium-high roast and used it in an espresso machine, you would make a less-burnt, less cremated feel; more subtle flavors, much more refreshing, much subtler. You'd never go back to the high-roast coffee.

What you're really getting is lightness, complexity, and better flavors than you would with run-of-the-mill coffee. The closest flavor comparison is Jamaican Blue Mountain coffee.

What does the future hold then?
What I think will happen is, projects like ours will help to develop not just the coffee industry but coffee drinking culture in Havana. Part of that project is to set up a chain of high-quality coffee shops in a chain of music shops in Cuba that already exists. I think what's happening ties in with what's happening with Cuban culture more generally. Currently, the closest thing to a specialty coffee place that exists in Havana is a government-run place called Café El Escorial in Habana Vieja; it has a small coffee roaster. But the food and drink is emerging from the socialist era and beginning to flourish. I don't think that you can necessarily get superb coffee in Havana at the moment. But I'm sure things will develop in future years. ∎

VIVA LA EVOLUCION

--

Writing by Christopher Baker
Photography by Daniela Velasco

Twenty-three years have passed since I first visited Cuba. Time enough for the rust-heap classic cars to finally croak. Strange, then, how many are looking better than ever—though most are Frankenstein-like automotives cobbled together from motley parts. I could say the same of coffee, which is still being stretched with *chícharo*, or roasted chickpea. Such is reality for penurious Cubans forced to rely on the meager government rations that, per adult, is comprised of only four ounces of adulterated ground Vietnamese beans each month.

Two decades ago, street cafes didn't exist in Havana. Even electricity was rationed from sundown to sun-up, due to nightly *apagones* (blackouts) following the collapse of the Soviet Union, then Cuba's main benefactor. The USSR's demise in 1991 spelled the slow decline of the Cuban government's guarantees of a decent egalitarian diet for all, and the onset of the Special Period, known to Cubans as "*el tiempo de los flacos*," or "time of the skinny people." I'm still pained by the scratch-and-sniff memory of frail Habaneros scavenging through reeking garbage; of memories of climbing dark, mildew-dank stairwells only to be greeted warmly with thimble-size *tazas* of harsh chickpea-laden coffee barely sweetened for lack of sugar, which I accepted with guilty gratitude.

The coffee shops that now grace the colonial plazas percolated slowly as tourism pulled Cuba from crisis. In the mid-1990s, state-run Al Cappuccino opened on Plaza de Armas as one of only a handful of places where you could actually buy an espresso or cappuccino (at least when the machines worked). Its atmosphere, alas, was as stale as a week-old *croissant*.

Then, in April 1997 Pain de Paris opened on Parque Central, with glass cases displaying fresh *bûchettes, éclairs, lonjas de almendros* (almond croissants), and other pastries that telegraphed a certain cosmopolitan air. I could almost imagine myself on the Champs-Élysées *merci à* Michel Villand's Francuba, his joint-venture French-Cuban company responsible for supplying Havana's chain of twelve Pain de Paris cafes.

Today, known as Pastelería Francesa, the original cafe is favored (as then) by tanned *jineteras* in body-tight clothing, sipping mochas. The clientele remains predominantly foreign and male.

Still, Che Guevara's presence clings on. His visage is everywhere, on billboards and murals soldered into the tropical grime. I once sipped on a cappuccino that had the ascetic communist revolutionary's face dusted in cinnamon onto the drink's frothy milk—the iconic image of Che in a five-starred beret photographed by Korda. It's funny where he shows up.

Today the city is energized by a newly unleashed entrepreneurial spirit. The government itself set the trend when, in 2009, in response to tourism's demands, visionary Eusebio Leal—the official historian of the city, in charge of restoration—opened the intimate Café El Escorial as the first (and still the only) *real* European-style cafe in town. It recreates the original, which functioned a century ago with a patio overlooking Plaza Vieja. Sharp aromas of freshly roasted beans from the Sierra Escambray spill from a Probat roaster and flavor the intimate place, with its whistling old brass-and-copper espresso machine, and a vast menu that features everything from *café au lait* to coffees mixed with rums, tequilas, and brandies.

I prefer squeezing into Dulcería Bianchini, hidden discreetly on Calle Sol, two blocks southeast of Plaza Vieja (a second outlet lies off Plaza de la Catedral). Barely half a dozen people can fit inside this cozy cubbyhole oozing emanations of an authentic French *patisserie*. Raised in Cuba to Swiss-Italian parents, owner Katia Bianchini dishes up too-good-to-resist cookies, cupcakes, and pains au chocolat, plus perfectly frothy cappuccinos and dulcet *cafecitos*—stove-top espressos served from an aluminum *cafetera*—with killer caramel-colored *espuma*, or sweet froth.

Don't believe anyone who tells you that Havana's cafe scene is sclerotic, or who says that cafes are for tourists only. The pace of change, felt by tourists and newly middle class locals alike, is suddenly frothier than a fresh cappuccino as entrepreneurs brew up intriguing new takes on cafes. Piscolabis Bazar-Café tempts you from cobbled Calle San Ignacio to browse exquisite *objets d'art* while you savor a fresh cuppa Joe. Café Tilín, on Trocadero in Centro Habana, serves up live music, from jazz to *nueva trova*. And for sheer elegance, Paris itself can't beat the chic, bohemian and cigar-friendly Siá Kará Café, behind the Capitolio on Barcelona. It's a veritable Cuban cafe Renaissance, and after twenty years of watching it slowly unfurl, I'd say better late than never. ∎

THE MOKA POT: A RECIPE

--

Recipes and photography by Adam Goldberg

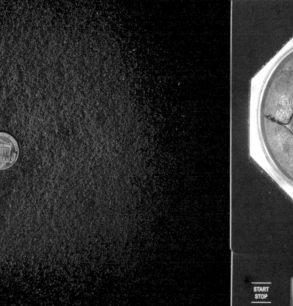

TOOLS:

Moka pot
Scale
Burr grinder
Carafe
Two serving cups
Non-metallic bowl (optional)
Rubber spatula (optional)
Measuring spoons

INGREDIENTS:

24 g fresh coffee beans ground so that grains are the size of fine sand, similar to the grind size for espresso.

280 g of water just below boiling point. Bring 500 g of water to a boil (extra water helps to maintain temperature), then let stand for 45 seconds.

2 tbsp white sugar (optional).

TO PREPARE:

1. Pour 280 g of just-boiled water into the bottom half of the Moka pot. Make sure the level of the water is below the steam vent.

2. Insert the metal portafilter into the bottom half of the Moka pot.

3. Add coffee, and use your finger in a sweeping motion to level out the coffee bed.

4. Screw together the Moka pot, tightly.

5. Place Moka pot over the stove on medium heat. Make sure that the handle of the pot is not over the flame.

6. After about two minutes, you will hear a puffing sound and a stream of coffee entering the upper chamber. Once the coffee turns from dark brown to light gold, remove from the stove with heat-resistant gloves.

7. Run the base of the Moka pot under cool running water to stop the extraction process.

8. Serve immediately or continue on to make *espumita*.

 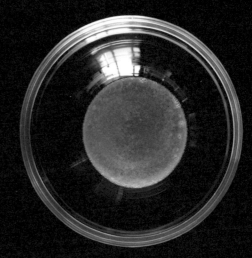

TO PREPARE ESPUMITA:

1. In a non-metallic cup or mixing bowl, add two tbsp of white sugar.

2. Add two tbsp of finished brewed coffee.

3. Beat coffee and sugar together with a rubber spatula, incorporating air, until a frothy *crema* begins to form. This is called the *espumita*.

4. Add the *espumita* to the bottom of serving cups.

5. Pour remaining coffee into cups and serve.

5 BROTHERS GROCERY AND SANDWICH SHOP
930 Southard Street
Key West, Florida, United States

304 O'REILLY
O'Reilly #304
Habana Vieja, La Habana

AL CAPPUCCINO
Obispo esquina Oficios
Habana Vieja, La Habana

AZUCAR
4820 Newport Avenue
San Diego, California, United States

BAR MARSELLA
Carrer de Sant Pau, 65
Barcelona, Spain

BUCHI CAFE CUBANO
2651 W 38th Avenue
Denver, Colorado, United States

CAFE BUSTELO FLAGSHIP STORE (Permanently closed)
2377 Collins Avenue
Miami, Florida, United States

CAFE EL ESCORIAL
Mercaderes #317, Plaza Vieja
Habana Vieja, La Habana

CAFETERIA LA MEJOR (Permanently closed)
191 Suydam Street
Brooklyn, New York, United States

CAFE MAMAINE
Calle L #206, entre Calles 15 y 17
Vedado, La Habana

CAFE TILIN
Águila esquina Trocadero
Habana Vieja, La Habana

CAFE O'REILLY
O'Reilly #203
Habana Vieja, La Habana

CAFETERIA
Aguacate esquina Obrapia
Habana Vieja, La Habana

CAFETERIA
Cerrado del Paseo #306
Habana Vieja, La Habana

CAFETERIA
Cuba #315
Habana Vieja, La Habana

CAFETERIA
Italia #513
Habana Centro, La Habana

CAFETERIA
Muralla #260
Habana Vieja, La Habana

CAFETERIA
Sol esquina Villegas
Habana Vieja, La Habana

CAFETERIA
Villegas esquina Lamparilla
Habana Vieja, La Habana

CAFETERIA EL CORTEZ
San José #266
Habana Centro, La Habana

CAFETERIA FERIA DE SAN JOSE
Alameda de Paula
Habana Vieja, La Habana

CAFETERIA LA CASITA CRIOLLA
Cristo #23
Habana Vieja, La Habana

CAFETERIA LA ESTRELLA
Aguacate esquina Muralla
Habana Vieja, La Habana

CAFETERIA LA FAMILIA
Bernaza #109
Habana Vieja, La Habana

CAFETERIA LA MILAGROSA
San Juan de Dios #220
Habana Vieja, La Habana

CAFETERIA LA MURALLA
Egido #309
Habana Centro, La Habana

CAFETERIA MI NIÑA
San Lazaro #213
Habana Vieja, La Habana

CAFETERIA SAINT JOHN'S
Calle 25 esquina Calle O
Vedado, La Habana

CAFETERIA TU PARADA
Avenida Desamparados #102b
Habana Vieja, La Habana

CUBA LIBRO
Calle 24 #304 y Calle 19
Vedado, La Habana

CUBAN COFFEE QUEEN
284 Margaret Street
Key West, Florida, United States

DULCERÍA BIANCHINI
Oficios esquina Avenida del Puerto, 12 Sol
Habana Vieja, La Habana

EL REY COFFEE BAR AND LUNCHEONETTE
100 Stanton Street
New York, New York, United States

HARRY'S BAR
Calle Vallaresso, 1323
San Marco, Venezia, Italy

HAVANA COFFEE WORKS
163 Tory Street
Wellington, New Zealand

HAVANA MIDNIGHT ESPRESSO
178 Cuba Street
Wellington, New Zealand

HOTEL NACIONAL
Calle 21 esquina O
Vedado, La Habana

INSTITUTO SUPERIOR DE ARTES (ISA)
Playa, La Habana

ISLAS CANARIAS
285 NW 27th Avenue #1
Miami, Florida, United States

LA BODEGUITA DEL MEDIO
Calle Empedrado entre Cuba y San Ignacio
Habana Vieja, La Habana

LA FÁBRICA DE ARTE CUBANO
Calle 26 esquina Calle 11
Vedado, La Habana

EL FLORIDITA
Obispo No. 557 esquina Monserrate
Habana Vieja, La Habana

LA TORRE
Calle M esquina Calle 17
Vedado, La Habana

LATIN AMERICAN MEDICAL SCHOOL (ELAM)
Carretera Panamericana Km 3 ½
Playa, La Habana

LES DEUX MAGOTS
6 Place Saint-Germain des Prés
Paris, France

LOS RIVALES
Avenida de Italia #517
Habana Vieja, La Habana

MUSEO NACIONAL DE BELLAS ARTES DE LA HABANA
Calle Trocadero entre Zulueta y Monserrate
Habana Vieja, La Habana

PAIN DE PARIS
Calle 25 #164 entre Infanta y Calle O
Vedado, La Habana

PASTELERIA FRANCESA
Paseo de Martí #411
Habana Vieja, La Habana

PISCOLABIS BAZAR-CAFE
San Ignacio #75 entre Callejón del Chorro y O'Reilly
Habana Vieja, La Habana

RESTAURANTE FLORIDITA
Obispo #557 esquina Monserrate
Habana Vieja, La Habana

RUSS & DAUGHTERS
179 East Houston Street
New York, New York, United States

SARAH LAWRENCE COLLEGE
1 Mead Way
Yonkers, New York, United States

SIA KARA CAFE
Calle Industria #502 esquina Calle Barcelona
Habana Vieja, La Habana

TENEMENT MUSEUM
103 Orchard Street
New York, New York, United States

UNIVERSITY OF HAVANA
San Lázaro y L. Municipio Plaza de la Revolución
Vedado, La Habana

CAFETERIA
Obrapia #461
Habana Vieja, La Habana

CAFETERIA
Calle Sol #411
Habana Centro, La Habana

CAFETERIA
Aguacate #268
Habana Vieja, La Habana

CAFETERIA
Compostela #401
Habana Vieja, La Habana

VERSAILLES
3555 Southwest 8th Street
Miami, Florida, United States

**

This list represents coffee shops visited, referenced, or interviewed on background for the making of *Drift*, Volume 3: Havana.

Volume 3: Havana
twitter/@driftny
facebook/driftny

Never miss an issue.
Subscribe online at: www.driftmag.com

instagram/@driftmag
twitter/@driftny
facebook/driftny